Oh,
What a Blow
That Phantom
Gave Me!

Oh, What a Blow That

Holt, Rinehart and Winston

Phantom
Gave Me!

EDMUND CARPENTER

New York · Chicago · San Francisco

Contents

Oh, what a blow that phantom gave me!
—*Don Quixote*

Worlds Within

ANGELIZATION

Electricity has made angels of us all—not angels in the Sunday school sense of being good or having wings, but spirit freed from flesh, capable of instant transportation anywhere. The moment we pick up a phone, we're nowhere in space, everywhere in spirit. Nixon on TV is everywhere at once. That is Saint Augustine's definition of God: a Being whose center is everywhere, whose borders are nowhere.

When a clerk stops waiting on us to answer a phone, we accept this without protest, yet it violates one of our most precious values—barbershop democracy. We accept it because pure spirit now takes precedence over spirit in flesh.

I knew a Californian who read his poetry aloud at parties until his friends learned to silence him. But when he played recordings of these same poems, everyone listened.

In New Guinea, when villagers ignore their leader, the government may tape-record his orders. The next day the assembled community hears his voice coming to them from a radio he holds in his own hand. Then they obey him.

Among the Ojibwa Indians, young people eagerly listen to tape recordings of their grandparents' stories, though they don't want to listen to the grandparents telling the same stories in person.

I've seen people practically break down a door to get to

a ringing phone, though the call was probably incidental. The phone is said to be the one thing that can interrupt intercourse.

I once saw a man passing a phone booth at the moment it rang. He hesitated & then, at the second ring, answered it. It couldn't possibly have been for him.

I copied down the numbers of several phones in Grand Central Station & Kennedy Airport, and called these numbers. Almost always someone answered. When I asked why they had answered, they said, "Because it rang."

Mordecai Richler tells how, when Lester Pearson took over as prime minister of Canada, he not only removed the emergency telephone linking his office with the White House, he concealed it so carelessly that when it rang one winter's morning in 1964, he couldn't find it. Paul Martin, then minister of external affairs, was with the prime minister at the time.

"My God," Martin exclaimed, "do you realize this could mean war?"

"No," Pearson replied. "They can't start a war if we don't answer it."

Some years ago in New Jersey, a mad sniper killed thirteen people, then barricaded himself in a house while he shot it out with the police. An enterprising reporter found out the phone number of the house and called. The killer put down his rifle and answered the phone. "What is it?" he asked. "I'm very busy."

More recently, a radio announcer called a bank that was being robbed. One of the robbers answered the phone & proceeded to give a radio interview, until he was interrupted by a policeman's shout: "Put up your hands! Put down that phone!" Putting up his hands meant being captured in flesh; putting down that phone meant being captured in spirit.

For Californians, February 9, 1971, was a day of combined cosmic and media theater. It began with an earthquake & included a total eclipse of the sun in the afternoon. Broadcasts throughout the day carried live conversations with astronauts

4

on the moon, including a warning to one not to pick up a rock. Cardiograms relayed to Houston indicated heart strain, something he himself didn't know.

That afternoon, in San Jose, a man successfully held up a TV bank, one of those drive-in banks with closed-circuit TV tellers. The robber pointed his gun at the TV set & warned he would start blasting away, so the bank paid off.

That night, on TV, an Air Force pilot said that air flak over Laos was "just like the Second World War movies on TV," and one newspaper reported that a welfare recipient, accused of wasting money on a color TV set, replied, "But I didn't want my children to grow up not knowing what color was."

A recent full-page magazine ad contained a photograph of a honeymoon lodge, complete with a heart-shaped, double-size tub surrounded by mirrors, and the caption: "We need mirrors to tell us we're really here. And the camera, courtesy of the thoughtful management, to remind us later when we try to recall just what it was like for those strangers ourselves."

In other words, for us, sexual experience is no longer the act but its mirrored or photographic image.

In the past, people called such images "unreal." The word "phony" comes from telephone: "He sounds like a phony to me." They experienced a great need to translate images back into flesh. Mark Twain made his living from public speaking; his readers wanted to see him. Dickens' fans flocked to hear him read works they already knew. Film stars were mobbed in public. Fans wanted to see the "real" Joan Crawford.

No more. TV stars walk the streets unmolested. People seem almost embarrassed to see them. They don't want to see Lorne Greene in a sports shirt on Maple Street. They expect him to stay in Bonanzaland, looking after those three boys, and they hurry home to watch him on TV.

THE SELF-SUFFICIENT IMAGE

Older people still experience the need to translate images into observed reality. When they travel, they want to see the Eiffel Tower or Grand Canyon exactly as they saw them first on posters. An American tourist in sneakers can cover the Louvre in six minutes, since there are only about seven things he recognizes—Winged Victory, Mona Lisa, etc.—and therefore wants to see. He can tell the cab driver to wait. Similarly, he can cover eleven capitals in two weeks, convinced he has missed nothing.

He does more than see the real Eiffel Tower. He photographs it exactly as he knows it from posters. Better still, he has someone photograph him in front of it. Back home, that photograph reaffirms his identity within that scene.

This need to translate images into objective reality has been a hidden factor in advertising: encountering only the image, people felt the need to acquire the product, not for its own sake but to complete & validate the ad. Similarly, they translated political images into votes.

Unlike their parents, the young are less anxious to validate images by reference back to observable reality. That need arose largely from conditions unique to literacy, and literacy exercises little control in their lives.

Today's images are often self-sufficient. We now have

ads that give more satisfaction than their products. Conceivably there doesn't even have to be a product. Sometimes when we try to purchase a product advertised on TV, we're told, "It's not yet in distribution," which probably means not yet in existence since consumer interest is often tested prior to production.

In government this is called a "press leak," though it's obviously not a "leak," having been planted in the news to test public response. In other words, it's possible to achieve the effect of a product or act without having either.

"Oh, what a beautiful baby!" exclaimed a neighbor.

"That's nothing," replied the mother. "You should see his photograph!"

MEDIA IDENTITIES

Eddie (Popeye Doyle) Egan, a narcotics detective who was the prototype for the character of Popeye Doyle in the film *The French Connection*, "readily acknowledged that the two Popeyes were one. 'I don't do it. Popeye Doyle throws the book away and he fights crime.' Neither Mr. Egan nor his agent, who was monitoring the conversation, seemed to notice he had assumed the fictional character."

New York Times, December 4, 1971

A Mexican-American seized a jet over Arizona and forced the pilot to fly to Los Angeles, where the hijacker held a television news conference. "He then surrendered, as he promised."

Washington Post, April 24, 1972

Joseph Gallo, reputed Mafia leader, was scheduled to give the keynote address before the A. J. Liebling Counter-Convention of Publishers. His topic: "The Image of Joe Gallo, in the Press and as I See It." However, he was murdered a few days before the conference opened.

"Gallo's sister, Mrs. Carmellia Fiorella, sobbing over her brother's body, said, 'He tried to change his image—that's why this happened.' She was treated for shock."

New York Times, April 8, 1972

WILL THE REAL ALICE PLEASE STEP FORWARD

"This image (seemingly animated) walks with them in the broad Day-light; and if they are employed in the delving, harrowing, Seed-sowing or any other Occupation, they are at the same time mimicked by the ghostly Visitant. Men of the Second Sight . . . call this reflex-man a Co-walker, every way like the Man, as his Twin brother and Companion, haunting as his Shadow."

—Kirk, *Secret Commonwealth*, 1691

NBC-TV broadcast a picture of Lyndon B. Johnson sitting transfixed in front of three television sets, each with a different image of LBJ.

CBS-TV broadcast the picture of an ancient Jack Benny on a TV talk show, in the studio, watching a movie of an elderly pajama-clad Jack Benny, at home, watching an old movie, on TV, in which a young Jack Benny, in the Orient, makes love to Dorothy Lamour.

MEDIA WITHDRAWAL

Those who find the physical & social environments too demanding, too messy, sometimes seek to live, as far as possible, within media environments.

Arthur Bremer, the would-be assassin of George Wallace, wrote in a school essay: "I would like to think that I was living with a television family and there was no yelling at home and no one hit me."

Recently at a U.S. Army base in Germany, the commanding officer attributed the high divorce rate among his troops to the lack of English-language TV. "That means a soldier and his wife have got to talk to each other in the evenings, and suddenly they discover they really don't like each other."

I saw a girl, on video tape, talking directly into the camera:

GIRL: Let me tell you how much I love you. . . .

MALE VOICE (interrupting): Tell *me*, not the camera.

GIRL: I can express myself better this way. . . .

MALE VOICE: Look, if we can't talk to each other, maybe we shouldn't marry.

GIRL: It isn't that I don't love you. I do. But in real life you always direct me. With your eyes. This way I can tell you how I *really* feel.

THE REEL WORLD

Tweedledum said to Alice, "You know very well you're not real."

"I *am* real!" said Alice, and began to cry.

"You won't make yourself a bit realer by crying," Tweed-ledee remarked. "There's nothing to cry about."

In preliterate societies, the separation of spirit from flesh is thought to occur in the surrealist realm of dream, art, ritual, myth. Daily life, in the field or on the hunt, is intensely sensate, with all senses alert & the spirit imprisoned in the body.

We reverse this. Our electronic workaday world divorces images from physical reality. As counterpoint, we turn physical reality into pastimes: the hippie world of sensate experience serves to balance the nonsensory spirit world of electronic media. Like natives, the young enjoy the best of both worlds, though it's hard to know which of these worlds to call "real."

On the surface, what could be more realistic than modern war, yet the Vietnam war employs more people in packaging & distributing its news than in combat. It's a media war, fought every night in our own parlors. The jungle war has been reduced to ritual only, played out by unknowing, sacrificial victims. Since we know these victims primarily as TV

11

actors, we're puzzled & frightened when in real life they bleed & die.

It's estimated that the ratio of noncombatants to actual fighters in 1914-18 was 12 to 1, at least as high as Vietnam. What has changed is the increased number assigned to "public relations."

According to the *New York Times*, June 21, 1972, a convoy, sent north from Saigon to help lift the siege of Anloc, consisted of "13 tanks, followed by several military jeeps, followed by eight reporters' cars and the Associated Press van, which resembles a bakery truck."

Suppose Vietnam went unreported in the news. "News" is what is reported; what isn't reported isn't news. Unreported events don't cease to exist, of course, they simply fall into an area devoid of social responsibility & moral restraint. "News" is information regarded as suitable for public attention, even public control. The Tonkin Gulf incident, which never occurred, was news, while MyLai, which did occur, went unreported. This was "All the News That's Fit to Print."

Suppose a person, even an entire group, is ignored by the media. Until recently, America was full of "invisibles." Blacks were ignored in literature. On radio, they became Amos 'n' Andy, played by two white men. On film, they became comic servants. They were never shown as cowboys, though in real life about a third of the post-Civil War cowhands were black. Deadwood Dick was black as coal, but on film he turned pink-cheeked & blue-eyed.

Blacks made their first public appearance on TV when they turned to violence. Suddenly they were no longer invisible. For one brief moment, they could be seen on TV. At which point, they were also seen for the first time on the streets.

But that moment passed quickly. The media image soon shifted from real blacks—unemployed, uneducated, hungry —to "media blacks"—well-dressed, professionally employed, college-educated. Real blacks once more became invisible.

12

But the impulse to translate TV into flesh is casual, not compelling. With print, great areas of sensory experience are felt to be missing. Readers experience a necessity to translate images into flesh & statements into actions. TV, by contrast, seems complete in itself. Each TV experience seems discrete, self-sufficient, true, of value in itself, judged & motivated & understood in terms of itself alone. Concepts such as causation & purpose appear irrelevant, basic only to the thinking of the past.

This sort of apprehension of being is familiar to anthropologists. Dorothy Lee, in *Freedom and Culture*, writes that Trobriand Islanders assumed "that the validity of a magical spell lay, not in its results, not in proof, but in its very being; in the appropriateness of its inheritance, in its place within the patterned activity, in its being performed by the appropriate person, in its realization of its mythical basis. To seek validity through proof was foreign to their thinking."

At the Chicago riots of 1968, the demonstrators shouted, "The whole world is watching!" And the whole world was. What they were watching was first-rate TV drama & they hadn't the slightest interest in translating this into response. Public reaction came only in print.

When Tweedledee told Alice, "You won't make yourself a bit realer by crying. . . . There's nothing to cry about," Alice replied, "If I wasn't real, I shouldn't be able to cry."

"I hope you don't suppose those are real tears?" Tweedledum interrupted in a tone of great contempt.

TV: A JOKING WORD

It was widely rumored among the young that John F. Kennedy didn't die in Dallas, but lived on, a vegetable kept alive in some secret clinic.

It was also rumored that the astronauts were identical twins or condemned criminals. This was part of the widely accepted belief that the moon shots were staged in northern Mexico. One of my own children assured me that the reason the moon rocks differed so much from what had been predicted was that they actually came from east Texas.

TV coverage of the moon visits & Kennedy's death may, in fact, have mirrored reality but, if so, this was exceptional. Taking TV as a whole, it would be difficult to refute the conviction of the young that this medium favors pure fiction. David Wolper, Hollywood's king of TV documentaries, recently said he was now "making his own old newsreels."

Such schoolboy pranks hardly compare to distortions arising from news treated as entertainment. Newsmen long ago discovered that news could be used as a hook from which to hang prejudices. They rarely reviewed current events or films or books; they merely ornamented opinions with them. For them, reality was an irrelevancy, something best avoided; what mattered was opinions about reality.

TV news favors this format. It offers cliché drama costumed as news. The commentator occupies the screen most of the time, though his visual appearance is totally irrelevant: Irrelevant to the news, but not irrelevant to the drama of the news hour, which is something utterly different, its own reality, with the commentator as star.

It takes someone out of the past to put all this in perspective. When a television director once suggested to Harry Truman that his tie was inappropriate for TV, Truman stared pityingly with those blue eyes for about ten seconds.

"Does it *really* matter?" he asked. "Because if while I'm talking about Korea people are asking each other about my necktie, it seems to me we're in a great deal of trouble."

Oscar Wilde once made up a joke about a biographer of Michelangelo who never mentioned his art. Wilde's joke is TV's policy. Educational TV loves to do profiles that "let viewers see the man," that is, deal with his loves & eccentricities, but ignore his genius, which may belong to a medium ill-suited for TV presentation. So TV presents specials on Einstein as a moral philosopher, Fitzgerald as an alcoholic & the Wright brothers as homosexuals.

I SAW A WOMAN FLAYED, AND YOU CANNOT IMAGINE THE DIFFERENCE IT MADE IN HER

Akiga, a Tiv of Nigeria who had received a Western education, heard that his father had killed & flayed one of Akiga's sisters, and given her skin to Akiga's brother to wear at a ceremonial dance. In his autobiography, Akiga tells how he went to the dance, but saw nothing more than his brother dancing, holding a woman's filter & his father's pipe. Yet the following day, the people who had gone to the dance were full of the story of how the brother Hilehaan had danced in his sister's skin. They weren't trying to deceive anyone; they were talking among themselves, discussing the important event they had witnessed. They had obviously perceived "the skin of the sister" (in the filter) "who had been flayed by her father" (in the father's pipe). Only the Western-minded Akiga saw just a filter & a pipe.

This case has been analyzed by the anthropologist Dorothy Lee, who noted that among the Tiv, as with nonliterate peoples generally, the symbol is regarded as an inseparable part of that which literate man believes it merely represents. Here the symbol participates in the total situation so that when the symbol alone is offered, it *conveys*—it doesn't create or evoke or apply—this value.

Literate man, however, regards the symbol as a neutral

16

label, something to be applied or changed at will. We say, "A rose by any other name would smell as sweet." We even take the name of God in vain on occasions when we would not welcome His presence, on the assumption the word doesn't convey the thing.

Only in isolated experiences, and these highly emotional, do we retain vestiges of this earlier way of thinking. At funerals, we avoid the emotionally charged word "death." We say, "He's no longer with us," or "He's been taken from us," not, "He's dead." That word would involve us in a reality we couldn't, at that moment, face. Yet we don't say, "Julius Caesar passed away," because we were never emotionally involved with him.

When I teach, if I must refer to bodily functions, I use the Latin terms for defecation & urination, not the better-known Anglo-Saxon ones. Otherwise, there is emotional discomfort.

The same applies to words for sex. Again, Latin is eminently suitable to the classroom since no one makes love in Latin these days.

We hesitate to destroy the portrait of someone we know, especially someone we love. I recall a macabre scene on one "Truth or Consequences" TV show where the guest, a woman sharpshooter, demonstrated her skill by hitting coins tossed into the air. But when stagehands brought out life-size photographs of her children & she was offered the grand prize if she would shoot out their eyes, she declined.

The connection between symbol & thing comes from the fact that the symbol—the word or picture—helps give the "thing" its identity, clarity, definition. It helps convert given reality into experienced reality, and is therefore an indispensable part of all experience.

It's not easy to experience the unfamiliar, the unnamed. We say, "If I hadn't seen it with my own eyes, I wouldn't have believed it," but the phrase really should be, "If I hadn't believed it with all my heart, I wouldn't have seen it."

We might say that the pencil I hold in my hand is a pencil

no matter what I call it in French or Chinese or even if I know no name for it. But is that true? A Maidu Indian, as Lee points out, gives no recognition to the pencil as object; instead he perceives the specific act of the hand—in this case the act of pointing with a pencil—and expresses this as "to point with a long thin instrument" (such as a pencil, a straight pipe, a cigarette, or a stick).

There are other people who see the pencil as an extension of the hand and express themselves accordingly.

And so we must ask ourselves, is it a pencil before I call it a pencil, or does it become a pencil in part through my naming it? Any word is far more than just a label, a decal, applied or removed at will. It contains meanings & associations & values which help give the thing its identity.

Even in science the observer is recognized as enmeshed in observed fact. Newton may have been confident that "facts" have a stable eternity outside the contaminating range of our psyche, but we are less confident. We accept that culture & language & other man-made patterns alter experience. Even to observe is to alter, and to define & understand is to alter drastically.

The so-called real world turns out to be not nearly so independent of human consciousness as was once thought. Even the most basic categories of grammar cannot be assumed to be universal. It's natural for us to conjugate & decline from singular to plural, because we begin with the one and go on to the many. Yet the Wintu Indians of California, as Dorothy Lee points out, recognize & perceive first the group and only secondarily the delimited one. They conjugate & decline from plural to singular and sometimes make no linguistic distinction between the one & the many or between the particular & the general.

Once when he was doing fieldwork among the Tikopia of the South Pacific, the British anthropologist Raymond Firth saw several women assembled during a ceremonial cycle. He asked what the women were doing, and was told, "The Atua Fafine [the chief Goddess] it is she."

For all of Firth's effort, it's impossible for him to make this sound logical & acceptable to people who know that ten women are plural; who learn from early childhood that $1 + 1 = 2$; and who, when they decline & conjugate, start with one & go to many.

Language does more than label: it defines; it tells not only what a thing is, but also its relation to other things. I may say that this pencil is lying *on* the table, making both pencil & table nouns, separate objects, with *on* indicating their relationship. But a Wintu would say, "The table lumps," or, if there were several things on the table, "The table lumps severally." The Wintu and I experience different realities, not simply the same reality in different ways.

What I've said of language applies to all media. It's often been noted that those who most enjoy ads, already own the products. Ads increase participation & pleasure; they help define experiences. A product without advertising can be, for many people, a nonexperience. And a thought or event that is excluded from all media, or that doesn't lend itself kindly to any available medium, is difficult to experience, even more difficult to convey.

SENSORY PROFILES

All peoples have the same senses, though not all use them alike. Eskimos have the same eyes I do, but, though my vision is 20/20, they spotted seals long before I did & continued to watch them long after the seals had disappeared from my sight.

Any sensory experience is partly a skill & any skill can be cultivated.

Charlie, blind since the age of two, spoke with a West Virginia drawl: "Well, my daddy and me enjoyed deer huntin' every fall. I got to know the sound—twigs breaking— even the weight, just by the way it sounded. My daddy sure was surprised when I got the deer first. He hadn't seen. . . ."

Charlie had worked hard to learn to shoot accurately by sound. He used a can with a few pebbles for a target, swinging it just enough to hear.

Wilfred Thesiger, in *Arabian Sands*, tells of a desert Bedouin reading camel tracks:

A few days later we passed some tracks. I was not even certain they were made by camels, for they were much blurred by the wind. Sultan turned to a grey-bearded man who was noted as a tracker and asked him whose tracks these were, and the man turned aside and followed them for a short distance.

20

Then he jumped off his camel, looked at the tracks where they crossed some hard ground, broke some camel-droppings between his fingers and rode back to join us. Sultan asked, "Who were they?" and the man answered, "They were Awamir. There were six of them. They have raided the Junuba on the southern coast and taken three of their camels. They have come here from Sahma and watered at Maghshin. They passed here ten days ago."

It's simply a question of training, though that training isn't simple. Reading tracks involves far more than just knowing where to look. Everything smelled, tasted, felt, heard, can be as relevant as anything seen. I recall being out with trackers once and when I stooped to scrutinize the trail, they stepped back, taking in the whole. Interpenetration & interplay of the senses are the heart of this problem.

No sense exists in total isolation. Run water into the bath while switching the light on & off—the sound appears louder in darkness & its location is easier to determine. Teach a soldier to strip & reassemble his rifle, then ask him to do it blindfolded & you will find he almost always does it faster without sight. Taste & smell seem stronger in the dark, which may be why good restaurants are candlelit. Darkness certainly makes love-making more interesting.

All peoples control their senses, though not always consciously. In our culture, librarians post signs reading SILENCE; concertgoers close their eyes; museum guards warn, "Don't touch!" Most of us know someone who puts on his glasses before talking on the phone.

West African dancers & singers close their eyes partially or wholly. The masks they wear are similarly carved. Masks with open, staring eyes are rare & usually covered by hanging hemp or fur. Sight is deliberately muted.

"If you paint," said Picasso, "close your eyes and sing. Painters," he added, "should have their eyes put out like canaries, so they'll sing better."

It's easier to discover a hidden design if you squint so that your eyelashes cloud your vision. This is especially true

21

in the case of visual puns where two or more images utilize one design. Only one image may be apparent at first, but cloud your vision & the second image suddenly appears while the first disappears.

I think a great deal of preliterate art is designed by artists who mute sight and that this art is viewed by audiences who perceive it in semidarkness or through half-closed eyes. Native house interiors are often dark. Ceremonies outside are frequently held at night by firelight. Costumed performers, which may include just about everyone, are generally masked, with restricted vision, and even when their faces aren't covered, they frequently lower their eyelids, even close their eyes.

When we put primitive art on museum display, isolated, on a pedestal, against a white background, under intense light, we violate the intention of the maker & create an effect far removed from the original.

Muting sight must have been particularly true of cave art. Paleolithic man worked in the darkness of caverns, his paintings illuminated by flickering torches.

Hans Arp, the contemporary artist, drew his curved, interpenetrating lines, which so closely resemble certain Paleolithic drawings, with half-closed eyes. In describing this experience, he wrote: "Under lowered lids, the inner movement streams untainted to the hand. In a darkened room it is easier to follow the guidance of the inner movement than in the open air. A conductor of inner music, the great designer of prehistoric images, worked with eyes turned inwards. So his drawings gain in transparency; open to penetration, to sudden inspiration, to recovery of the inner melody, to the circling approach; and the whole is transmuted into one great exhalation."

Muting sight can increase awareness in other senses, especially hearing. The opposite effect—blotting out other sensory experience—can be achieved by heightening the input of a single sense. Dentists use high-pitched sound to numb pain. Turn up your hi-fi & you may not smell the burning toast until much too late.

One can turn sound up by turning sound inward. In New Guinea, singers sometimes plug one or both ears, producing an "inner voice" effect where pitch is felt as vibration. Singers determine pitch by feel. The experience is not unlike rock music which one feels, often through the entire body.

What I've said of muted sight & magnified sound are but two examples from a wide range of sensory patterns or profiles. Man everywhere programs his inner senses with the care & genius with which he programs his outer environment.

FEELING WITH THE EYE

A remarkable change took place in the human condition with the rise of Euclidian space, three-dimensional perspective, and, above all, the phonetic alphabet. Each of these inventions favored the eye at the expense of all other senses. The value accorded the eye destroyed the harmonic orchestration of the senses & led to an emphasis upon the individual experience of the individual sense, especially the sense of sight. Where other senses were employed, it was with the bias of the eye.

The eye is like no other sense. When used in isolation, it perceives a flat, continuous world without intervals. Yet it also favors only one thing at a time: it focuses on a *part*icular & abstracts it from a total situation. To connect these fragments, literate man built mental bridges. He spoke of a "row of trees" or a "circle of stones," when neither row nor circle existed except in his mind & language. He favored the "story-line" & arranged his thoughts "seriously," that is, serially. From this came the scanning eye of the reader & much else besides: lineality, causality, temporality, ultimately much of what we call Western civilization.

Western man not only emphasized sight, but a special kind of sight, "pure sight," divorced from all other senses. "At first sight" the world looks flat, as if it were no more

24

than meaningless patches of light & color jumbled into a quiltwork. Infants born without arms or legs can never see in depth. Depth is discovered by touch, then married to sight. The eye caresses *over* objects.

Tactility converts the flat world of sight into the three-dimensional world of bodies. One by one, objects grow out of this chaotic world and remain unmistakably separate when identified. Patients, blind from birth, on whom vision has been bestowed by an operation, at first shrink from the welter of additional stimulation & from the flat continuity of the world they see. In 1964, in Sicily, five brothers—all blind from birth—each acquired sight following an operation. Months later, they were photographed holding on to one another, with downcast eyes, as the lead brother *felt* his way through the doorway of their home. It took time & effort before they once more recognized the objects around them as separate items.

The world of the blind is a world of three-dimensional bodies existing in emptiness. Test this yourself: move about the room with eyes closed—suddenly, without warning, you will bump into some object. Emptiness combines with sudden interface. All encounters become abrupt. "To the blind, all things are sudden." Without sight, connections are lacking: all the gradations, shadings, & continuities of the visual world are gone.

Artists *visually* convey the sense of touch in a variety of ways. Renoir painted a woman's body as the hand feels it, not as the eye sees it. Leonardo's multiline sketches of women & children also belong to the hand, not the eye.

In the same sense, artists create hard-edge art, that is, abrupt edges with intervals. When Gertrude Stein met Picasso in Paris, around 1905, he asked her to obtain American comic strips for him. He was studying Japanese prints at the time, but found in comic strips clearer examples of interface & interval which interested him so much. It was at this time he began the study of African tribal art.

Most tribal art is hard-edge art. So is children's art. A

Vancouver filmmaker provided young children with the means to make animated films. The result was nearly 200 films of WHAM! BANG! with figures appearing, disappearing. There were no characters in the ordinary sense: no shadings, no gradations, just abrupt encounters á la Batman of hard-edge, cartoon art. Hard-edge art is a visual presentation, but the experience it evokes or conveys isn't visual; it's tactile. It's full of abrupt encounters—sudden interfaces, then emptiness.

When you have interface & emptiness, you have happenings. In the world of happenings, surfaces & events collide & grind against each other, creating new forms, much as the action of dialogue creates new insights. It's the world of all-at-onceness where things hit each other but where there are no connections.

Not only artists & writers, but also composers use this combination of hard-edge & interval to convey the experience of touch. Edgard Varèse writes: "Electronics has given music a new dimension and a new freedom. My music is based on the movement of unrelated sound masses which I always conceived as moving simultaneously at different speeds, and I looked forward to the time when science would provide the means of realization. Now, thanks to electronics, such unrelated metrical simultaneity is at last possible."

Much contemporary music favors interface & interval, in contrast to the acoustic continuity of symphonic music. These techniques are basic to the poetry of Pound & Eliot, as they were for the Symbolists. Above all, Joyce took over the art of the interval.

He used interval & interface as a means of retrieving that fantastic wealth of perception & experience stored in ordinary language. Dispensing with the storyline became a means of instant grasp of complex wholes.

The scanning eye is offended by both intervals & abrupt encounters. It favors continuity. It builds bridges in the mind to create a smooth, uninterrupted flow from word to word, thought to thought. Joyce dynamited that freeway, leaving

26

gaping intervals & massive roadblocks. Suddenly it was no longer possible to skim the page: the reader fell between words, struggled over others, and soon he was swarming all over them, experiencing them in new ways, going right inside them, deciphering riddles, discovering hidden dimensions, releasing imprisoned energies.

SEEING IN THE ROUND

To depict a whole object on a flat surface, literate man employs three-dimensional perspective: he shows only that surface visible from a single position at a single moment. In short, he fails.

In contrast, native artists of British Columbia represented a bear, say, in full face & profile, from back, above & below, from within & without, all simultaneously. By an extraordinary mixture of convention & realism, these butcher-draftsmen skinned & boned, even removed the entrails, to construct a new being, on a flat surface, that retained every significant element of the whole creature.

HEARING WITH THE EYE

The eye focuses, pinpoints, abstracts, locating each object in physical space against a background. In contrast, the ear accepts music from all directions simultaneously.

The essential feature of sound is not its location, but that it *be*. We say, "The night shall be filled with music," just as the air is filled with fragrance. We wrap ourselves in music.

We can also wrap ourselves in art, even two-dimensional art. Visual puns, where two or more images coexist within a single design, are the visual counterpart of jazz with its interweaving rhythms.

Jacket designs for jazz records often use paintings by Klee & Miró. Both painters structured space by all the senses, particularly sound. Both state that they painted under the guidance of the ear. Correspondences between their paintings & jazz are hardly coincidental.

Klee said his works owed more to Bach & Mozart than to any of the masters of art. He wanted art "to *sound* like a fairy tale," to be a world in which "things fall upward."

"Right now," said Miró, "I'm in a Bach mood. Tomorrow it could be Stockhausen. I'm very fond of the Beatles, too."

I don't regard as accidental the close parallels between Eskimo art & the work of Klee & Miró. In each there is

29

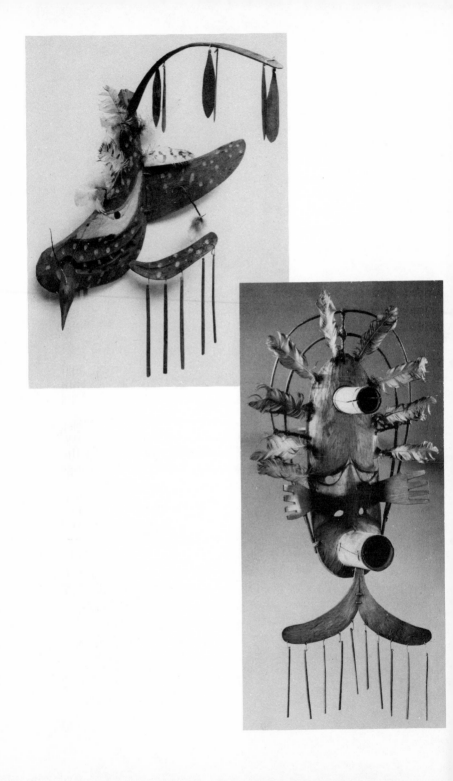

a structuring of space by all the senses. Consider the case of Kuskokwim masks neglected by Western scholars until discovered by the surrealists Ernst, Breton, Matta, and Donati in 1943. The masks are complex mobiles with extensions & moving parts, like dissected Mirós reassembled in three dimensions. No borders freeze, imprison. Instead, each mobile, obedient to an inner impulse, asserts its own identity, unhampered by external restraints.

Acoustic space isn't pictorial, boxed-in, framed: it's resonating, in flux, creating its own dimensions moment by moment. It's a world in which the eye hears, the ear sees, & all the five & country senses join in a concert of interweaving rhythms.

THE MEANINGFUL EXPERIENCE

Last year [1806] one of the Osages, then in Washington for
the first time, was taken to see the frigates and gun boats
in the Eastern branch—when the Captain of the Port made
every shew he could in order to astound him, but all in vain:
he was even taken to the gun boat in which the cannon is
discharged by pulling a string and without letting him know
what was to happen, the string was put in his hand and he
was told to pull it, he did so and altho' the sudden sound,
one might have supposed, would have startled him, he did
not move a muscle.—Sir Augustus J. Foster

The case is not isolated. It was a favorite joke, in many
parts of the world, to fire a cannon next to an unsuspecting
native. If there were crowds, there was generally consterna-
tion. But with single individuals, again & again we have
reports of men totally unmoved.

Dr. Jean Itard's famous account of a "wild" boy found
in the forests of Aveyran in southern France, in 1799, tells
how, when a door was suddenly slammed, the boy didn't
move. For a time it was thought he must be deaf, until
one day he was observed listening to the sound of a mouse
in the leaves.

A child, sleeping in a pram, may ignore the roar of a
diesel truck, but respond to its mother's whisper.

We respond only to what we recognize, to what holds
meaning for us.

32

TRANSLATION

Translation is generally imperialistic, at best producing a creative hybrid, but more frequently destructive, turning what is translated into hash or comedy or a mirrored image of the translator. Translation rarely achieves the translucency that the word implies.

Obviously, if the underlying structure of the translator's language, medium, and sensory profile are all compatible with the form translated, it is easier to retain the effect of the original.

We could say of a Rembrandt: this is a portrait of a man with a golden helmet. But, as George Steiner writes in *Language and Silence*, absolutely nothing that can be *said* about Franz Kline's painting *Chief* will be pertinent to the habits of linguistic sense. "The patches of color, the skein of wire, or the aggregates of cast iron seek to establish reference only to themselves, only inwards." A de Kooning canvas has no subject of which one can render a verbal account. It bypasses language & seems to play directly on the nerve ends.

The same applies to much contemporary dance, film & music, especially electronic music. When we ask the contemporary artist to explain himself in words, he refers us back to his work. Isadora Duncan said, "If I could tell you what it meant, there would be no point in dancing it." She was reluctant to translate her efforts into English, a medium whose

structure was wholly different from, and incompatible with, her particular dancing.

Translating Rembrandt into English or any Standard Indo-European language is possible, I believe, because of a correspondence in structures. All Standard Indo-European languages separate time & space through grammar; Rembrandt separated time & space through three-dimensional perspective. Both favor self-expression, self-portraiture. What Montaigne wrote, Rembrandt painted.

In art history, similarities of design are generally explained as being the result of either convergent evolution or diffusion or genius. That these similarities might arise from similarities in life styles & sensory profiles &, above all, in deep structures of media, none of which is necessarily related to evolution or diffusion or greatness, is less frequently considered.

Glenn Miller said he could always tell when he & his band were really "in the groove" during World War II, because when this happened, the fringe of natives who were standing around outside the GI's would all begin to move in rhythm with the music.

SYNCHRONIZING THE SENSES

At the Chicago World's Fair in 1932, United States Marines competed with Radio City Rockettes in precision marching. As the marines' heels came down, the Rockettes' toes went up. All movements were synchronized.

When literate man dances, he keeps step to the music. His marching bands have drum majors; his orchestras, conductors. Every player is synchronized to a single beat.

In West Africa, every player has his own downbeat. There may be as many as five simultaneous rhythms—the melody & four percussion parts. Three rhythms are widely common in preliterate music: melody, handclapping & tapping the feet. The individual performs all three simultaneously, though not in synchronization. The combined result is neither chaos nor conformity, but a complex pattern of interweaving rhythms, each with its own integrity.

When Walt Disney added sound to animated films, he synchronized the two exactly: French horns went RUUMP when volcanoes erupted. UPA artists couldn't afford such costly sound effects, so they experimented with existing music until they found something that "worked." The result was films with music & picture coexisting, each with its own integrity. In contrast, music in Disney films was subservient to the visual story, little more than sound effects.

Synchronizing the senses means one sense dominates all others. Under literacy, that sense is sight. Other senses are muted or used with the bias of the eye. Sight has a natural bias toward detachment, creating the detached observer, whereas sound has an opposite bias: it surrounds, involves —one steps into it.

Literate peoples experience sound as if it were visible: they listen *to* music. Nonliterates merge *with* music. Far from being detached, they become involved participants, immersing themselves totally in it.

SIGHT, THE GREAT VALIDATOR

Literacy orchestrated the senses under a single conductor: sight. It enthroned sight to the point where it alone was trusted. All truth was expected to conform to observed experience.

Aristotle, in the first sentence of *Metaphysics*, says, "Of all the senses, trust only the sense of sight." Plato tells us there is a hierarchy of senses, with sight at the top, touch at the bottom.

Sight became supreme & all other senses became subservient to it. Literate man said, "Seeing is believing"; "Believe half of what you see and nothing of what you hear"; "I'm from Missouri—show me." For him, the observable object or act was the reality: truth was determined by reference to it.

He replaced mythology with history & sent biblical scholars off to the Holy Land to dig up Noah's ark & the walls of Jericho. His art imitated nature, that is, optical reality: people expected artists to paint what they saw. They agreed with Winston Churchill who said, "When I paint a cow, I want it to look like a cow."

Dreams were dismissed until Freud announced they were really historical accounts concealed in secret code. Court evidence was largely direct evidence, preferably the eye-witness

38

account: this was considered "the truth, the whole truth, and nothing but the truth."

Written music became increasingly linear & narrative. Even early mathematics, with certain notable exceptions, was anchored in material experience. Above all, early science was descriptive & classificatory: it dealt with the observable & measurable, and therefore was regarded as the most refined method for determining truth. Literate languages stressed the world of observable surfaces. The eye of the reader scanned life as well as print.

THE UNIVERSE AS BOOK

It was a commonplace in Scholasticism that God created two books: the world & the sacred Scriptures. Life was thought to follow the format of the book & the book became the organizing principle for all experience.

Even as a written manuscript, the book served as model for both the machine & bureaucracy. That is, it encouraged a habit of thought that divided experience into specialized units & organized these serially & causally. Translated into gears & levers, the book became machine. Translated into people, it became army, chain of command, assembly line, etc.

By organizing society in the format of the book, the ancients organized specialists into elaborate social machines capable of building pyramids or colonizing conquered lands.

The book served as model & impetus for many of Western man's most basic thoughts. Certainly the book was ideally suited for presenting a number of these. "History," says George Steiner, "is a language-net thrown backwards." More specifically, history is a book.

Theories of evolution & progress belong, almost exclusively, to book culture. Like a book, the idea of progress was an abstracting, organizing principle for the interpretation & comprehension of an incredibly complicated record of human experience. It arranged events in a line, causally: the individual was thought to move along that line, like the reader's eye, toward a desired goal.

Nearly all experience, all reality, it was thought, lay within the confines of language. Language, in turn, was structured by the book. Thus, nearly the whole of Western culture was organized around one sense: the eye; expressed in one medium: language; and structured according to one model: the book.

The all-seeing eye of God, believed to control all celestial bodies & all life, was really the eye of literate man. Western civilization synchronized nearly all experience, all perception to this single model & organized the universe according to the book.

Literate man lived in a universe, not a bi-verse or a multi-verse, but a verse obedient to a single drummer. "Whether in the Amazonian forest or on the ridge of the high Andes," wrote Alexander von Humboldt, the great geographer, "I was ever aware that *one* breath, from pole to pole, breathes *one* single life into stones, plants and animals and into the swelling breast of man."

Monotheism in religion & uniformity in classical science were mild dictatorships compared to the dictatorship of the eye. In fact, both may have been by-products of it. Alfred North Whitehead said science could have come only out of the strict monotheism of Christianity, but it seems more likely the primary source was literacy, not religion.

PLAY IT BY EAR

In preliterate societies, experience is often arranged by a sense life that represses visual values. When visual models are introduced into such societies, they often have great power.

Renaissance pilgrims from rural villages were taken on cathedral tours to view biblical paintings—to see what hitherto they had known only by ear.

"The function of medieval art," writes Marshall McLuhan, "was to involve all of the senses in order to convince." Renaissance science reduced certainty to one sense mode: sight. Newton was first branded a medieval mystic when his theory of gravity presented a nonvisual bond & reversed downward gravity by outward gravity. However, his very visual example of a falling apple made his theory acceptable to the many.

People quickly understood Darwin's theory of human descent when they saw that apes in the zoo did, in fact, resemble relatives.

We converted statistics to charts & heartbeats to graphs. Scientific theories which failed to lend themselves to visual illustration were slow to gain popular acceptance. Mendel was ignored for thirty-five years.

But today, once again, visual models are often irrelevant. "What Sony hears, is," reads a recent ad.

SEPARATE REALITIES

In the novel *In the Region of the Ice*, a nun who teaches literature, Sister Irene, speaks of a brilliant, mad student. "'I'm very grateful to have him in class. It's just that . . . he thinks ideas are real.' Sister Carlotta, who loved literature also, had been forced to teach grade-school arithmetic for the last four years. That might have been why she said, a little sharply, 'You don't think ideas are real?' Sister Irene acquiesced with a smile, but of course she did not think so: only reality is real."

Under literacy, particularly print, all experience was subject to a single code. Inner experiences were expected to conform to outer perceptions. Any failure of correspondence was regarded as hallucination. The individual who failed in this was thought to be living in a world of self-deception.

Spatial metaphors were employed to describe the inner psychological states of tendency, duration & intensity. Literate man said, "I cannot *come to grips with* your thought because its *level* is *over* my head, our *views* being so *far apart* I *lose touch* with what you are *trying to make clear*."

Surrealist art was wholly unacceptable. It was *non*sense.

Even dreams were expected to resemble waking life. When they failed to do so, they were dismissed as temporary mental aberrations, unworthy of attention.

Freud advised his readers to take dreams seriously because, he said, they are proper history; one need only translate them out of their secret code into waking, historical experiences and then they will all "fall in line" & "make sense."

To the young today, however, the dream experience is its own reality, a separate reality: it doesn't need to be validated by translation into the historical world of sensory experience. It validates itself.

Similarly, they regard media as self-contained environments, having little correspondence with other realities or environments. TV is its own reality, radio its reality, film still another reality.

Each creates its own space, its own time. The clock on the "Today" Show has no hour hand.

When TV fans seek correspondence between TV & reality, reality often surrenders to TV. Recently two communities, each lying within the Salt Lake City broadcasting area, but in another time zone, petitioned the Department of Commerce for rezoning. They wanted clock time to conform to broadcast time.

The young in particular regard media environments as designs, patterns—what William Blake called "sculptures"—states that have no separate physical existence. We pass temporarily into one or another & when in any one, it seems overpoweringly real & all other states shadowy. We imagine, of course, that any state we are in is physically real. This makes it splendidly attractive. It doesn't occur to us that only our spirits can enter these realms, and that events experienced there can never be tested against observed reality.

I think this is one reason the young find nothing incongruous about conflicting reports in the press, radio, TV, etc.

That same absence of concern with the contradictory, on the part of preliterate peoples, led the French philosopher Lévy-Bruhl to write an entire book in which he concluded that natives suffered from a "pre-logical mentality." He said they weren't bothered by the coexistence of contraries, but let mutually contradictory reports exist side by side. When we examine closely the examples he offered, we find many remarkably close to modern experiences.

I asked students who had seen the film *Patton* to read A. J. Liebling on Patton. Liebling points out that the press credited Patton with victories others achieved. The students enjoyed Liebling, just as they enjoyed the film, but not one mentioned contradictions. To them, each was its own reality. Each was self-contained. Neither validated nor invalidated the other.

Then I asked them to read a biography of Rommel, who as a tactician was certainly Patton's equal, but in habit mild-mannered, thoughtful of his men, an anti-Nazi who plotted to kill Hitler. This, too, they enjoyed & accepted. They didn't see that Rommel's life challenged the theme of the film that it takes bullies to win battles.

As a boy I was enormously impressed with Charles Laughton's performance in *Mutiny on the Bounty*. But when I read a book on Captain Bligh, which described him as a humane & able leader, and documented this historically, my faith in the film was shattered. Then I read a second book on the fifteen mutineers who, far from being noble martyrs, on Pitcairn Island turned into murderers, rapists, & alcoholics, with only one surviving. At this point the film, for me, became a total fraud.

Recently I showed this film to students & asked them to read both books. I even projected a contemporary portrait of Bligh, showing a small-featured gentleman of pleasant expression, not the heavy-browed sea dog of film fame. No one raised questions of accuracy.

When I raised such questions, they dismissed them. They refused to relate art forms outward, to take reality as arbiter.

To someone my age, this is disturbing. To the young, it's entirely appropriate. They regard the press & TV, in fact all media, the way they regard LP records: as separate worlds. They don't relate recorded music back to performance. That music exists *now*, with them in it. It's complete,

45

no mere shadow of some distant original. And it's doubtful, in any case, if there ever was, in any conventional sense, an original performance, especially where audience involvement becomes part of the performance.

One Christmas, President Eisenhower sent out cards bearing color reproductions of a watercolor he had painted on top of a drawing by a talented enlisted man from a photograph of the White House. Counting negatives, these cards must have been at least eight generations removed from "reality."

To the young, I suspect each version is a separate reality.

None of this, George Steiner tells me, applies to students in England or Europe. He regards it as an American phenomenon. Certainly the present ratio of telephones to world population remains minute. One can still hike in Northumberland or in an Alpine valley, right in the heart of industrial Europe, and encounter few electronic images. Even within the United States the pattern is not uniform.

But where electronic media prevail, they are the new environments. They even have the power to challenge language, man's earliest & perhaps most basic environment. TV deprives its viewers of speech. Those who live within it retreat from language. When Jean Piaget asked Swiss children, "What do you think with?" most replied, "The mouth." Children in the most diverse cultures make this association. It may, until recently, have been a universally held concept. But today, in the United States, there are reports of children who associate thinking with television.

WHN-1050 IS A PUT-ON.
EVERYBODY PUT ON WHN RADIO (OR ELSE!)

We don't read a newspaper: we step into it the way we step into a warm bath. It surrounds us. It environs us in information.

We wear our media. They are our real clothes.

Radio & TV bombard us with images, cover us tattoo-style: they clothe us in information, program us. At which point, nudity ceases to have meaning. Asked if she had anything on when posing for nude calendar shots, Marilyn Monroe replied, "The radio."

We come to know a thing by being inside it. We get an inside view. We step into the belly of the beast and that, precisely, is what the masked & costumed dancer does. He puts on the beast.

Traditionally in New Guinea, dancers in floral skirts & feather headdresses put on the jungle, wrapping themselves in their environment. They became one with the plants & animals.

Now they wrap themselves in information. Radio reclothes them.

We assume the role of our costume, our information. The public figure's image, detached from his body by electricity,

48

is transferred to ours. His spirit enters us, possesses us, displacing our private spirit. We wear his image, play his role, assume his identity. When Eisenhower suffered a heart attack, the stock market fell. On Moratorium Day in Washington, April 1971, tens of thousands of marchers, clothed in collective guilt, wore Lieutenant Calley masks.

In the preliterate world, spirit possession is thought to occur rarely, under circumstances fraught with mystery & danger. With us, it occurs daily, without wonder, free from examination.

MEMORY

No manuscript has been preserved of a set of *rimur* composed by the Icelandic author Sigurour Bjarnson in 1862. But, according to William Craigie, a younger brother learned them by heart at the age of fifteen, and at the same time noted the first line of each verse. Fifty-five years later, in Canada, and without having gone over them in his mind for thirty years, he dictated the whole of them, to the extent of 4,000 lines, and they were printed at Winnipeg in 1919.

This is a remarkable case, but by no means unique. Anthropological literature is full of examples of oral traditions drifting through time & space without significant loss. Societies we call primitive often have a quite staggering capacity of remembering. Certain American Indian myths can be traced to Asia, and there are Polynesian communities that can recite, straight off, family trees involving dozens of generations.

Oral people have excellent memories; literate peoples are what Joyce called "ABCED-minded." "Our memories," writes H. J. Chaytor, "have been impaired by print; we know that we need not 'burden our memories' with matter which we can find merely by taking a book off a shelf. When a large proportion of a population is illiterate and books are scarce, memories are often tenacious to a degree outside modern European experience."

Indian students learn a textbook by heart & reproduce it word for word in an examination room; sacred texts are preserved intact by oral transmission alone. It is said that if all written & printed copies of the *Rigveda* (about as long as the *Iliad* & *Odyssey* combined) were lost, the text could be restored from memory, at once, with complete accuracy.

In the late Middle Ages, the Inquisition found it was not enough to burn books. They constantly charged the Waldensians with knowing large portions of Scripture by heart. Other dissenters were said to have known the whole of the New Testament & parts of the Old Testament.

It's easier to recall poetry than prose, and easier still to recall song. But often, what is remembered most clearly is danced-song, learned by heart, then endlessly improvised. Learned "by heart" means the learner is totally involved, his heart or lungs being regarded as the seat of his soul, the place where all senses commingle & all memories live.

Forgetfulness rarely destroys, nor do improvisations mar, a song or dance learned in this way. Cases are common of men revealing songs they had neither sung nor heard for forty years, but remembered perfectly.

The term "oral tradition" is misleading, for generally all the senses are involved in such cases. There seems to be everywhere a natural tendency for the senses to interpenetrate & interplay, "the ear-bone connected to the eye-bone" creating a concert or orchestration in which the ear sees, the eye hears, one smells-tastes color, and all the senses engage in every experience.

An East Indian treatise of the sixth century A.D. describes a conversation in which a sage advises a king that he must first learn the theory of dancing before he can learn the whole meaning of art, since the law of dancing imply the principles that govern painting.

Bill Holm, a student of Northwest Coast Indian art & dance, speaks of "a certain physical satisfaction from the muscle activity involved in producing the characteristic line movement of this art" and the fact that "some of the most skillful artists of the southern Kwakiutl are also among the best dancers and song composers." He writes: "The constant flow of movement, broken at rhythmic intervals by rather sudden, but not necessarily jerky, changes of motion-direction, characterizes both the dance and art of the Northwest Coast."

Writing & print relieve a strain upon memory and give time for deliberate consideration. But they do far more than this: the sensory mechanics of reading, plus the value accorded to the eye at the expense of all other senses, destroy the harmonic orchestration of the senses and reduce each image to one sense or another. The result is that the experience cannot be "relived" in memory. It cannot be learned "by heart" since its unity has been shattered by translation into writing.

I see loss of memory as a by-product of literacy, specifically literacy's role in shattering sensory orchestration. One great advantage of memory loss is that one isn't burdened with masses of obsolete information: the mind is left free to process new data and get on to still more data. In a complex, changing culture, where the mind must process—not store—data, this is an indispensable asset.

But in preliterate cultures, where experience is often limited by geography & limited even more by culture, that culture is presented to its members as clichés, repeated over & over with only slight variation.

The binding power of the oral tradition is very strong. We speak of such societies as "closed societies," and, to a large extent, they are. Little breaks in from without. It's not unlike osmosis where the membrane keeps in, and lets in, desirable fluids, but excludes all that threaten, all that are alien.

I once naively thought my Eskimo hosts would be fascinated to hear about the remarkable world from which I came. In fact, they showed only irritation when I talked about it. If a tubercular Eskimo is taken from his igloo & put in a sanatorium in Brandon, Manitoba, or Hamilton, Ontario, and treated there for four years, gradually being given freedom to wander about the hospital & town, when he returns home, it's unlikely he will ever mention a single thing he witnessed or learned. The outside world is uncertain, dangerous, hostile—above all, alien, untranslatable.

Look at the content of European folksongs. What happens to the person when he leaves his village & valley? He drowns at sea or is hung as a highwayman or abandoned by a false lover or wanders alone through a hostile landscape. The message is clear: nothing good lies outside. The tribe may be small, the village smaller, but, like the child's world, it's complete. It contains enough ambitions & passions to fill the hollow pit of human desire. There's little reason to leave. There's less reason to tolerate intruders.

Little changes within. Yet memory is never fixed & lifeless. There is always improvisation. A singer may be able to reproduce a song after hearing it only two or three times, but his reproduction is never exact, nor are his later renderings always alike. He is free to improvise, never twice rendering the song exactly the same, as long as he never violates its grammar. What he faithfully reproduces, with absolute fidelity, is its underlying structure, that unseen grammar that determines its form & sets its style. We might compare it to learning a 5-times table: one can improvise indefinitely as long as one remains obedient to its rules. The whole point is not to memorize patterns, but to understand rules determining these patterns.

In New Guinea, in a remote native school taught by a local teacher, I watched a class carefully copy an arithmetic lesson from the blackboard. The teacher had written:

$$4 + 1 = 7$$
$$3 - 5 = 6$$
$$2 + 5 = 9$$

The students copied both his beautifully formed numerals & his errors. They were graded on their success in exact

reproduction. The difficulty, of course, wasn't merely that the memorized lessons lacked coherency & use, but that one couldn't go beyond them & improvise.

When I speak of my 5-times table, I don't mean mine to do with as I like, but mine as long as I am obedient to it. Artists & musicians may not be as conscious as mathematicians of the underlying rules that govern their fields, perhaps because these rules are not as explicit, but the rules of art & music are nevertheless there and the successful artist or musician obeys them. Obedience frees him to improvise, to play, to become involved creatively, repeating, repeating, repeating with endless variations.

This repeat/repeat of cliché may be the key to memory. There is a vital difference between variations which maintain the freshness of a style and changes which destroy & replace that style. Native art is often startlingly original to us, but in its own context, it is to the highest degree conservative & familiar. When we reproduce this art in books & this music on records, we usually edit it sharply. We delete what is repetitious, since it bores us, in favor of variety, which entertains us. But the originals themselves are highly repetitious. Their recitation provides a tribal beat, a common pulse, to which the group collectively responds.

Preliterate art is not unlike modern advertising, much of which is sung & all of which is highly repetitious. Advertising isn't designed to train perception & awareness, but rather to insist that consumers merge with images & products.

Such art isn't personal. It doesn't reflect the private point of view of an innovator. It's a corporate statement by a group. It's a public celebration. It lives within each member through memory, participation & improvisation.

In contrast, art involving a single sense & expressing a private view exists outside of the observer, in libraries & galleries where it can be studied.

Maurice Wilkins writes: "Art, higher learning, politics, economics—none of these activities today is properly related to human needs: all are fragmented. Like science, art has

become remote from living: it is not, as . . . in primitive societies, an integral part of our culture, existing in all aspects of life, in everyday matters, in religion. Art has become separate and specialized, understood only by a minority, segregated in galleries, museums and concert halls, and, like science, exploited for political and commercial ends."

COLLECTIVE UNCONSCIOUS

Alaskan Eskimo artists turned to dreams & trances for inspiration. They hoped to penetrate a house of knowledge which they believed lay beneath the sea. When they returned to the land of men, they carved likenesses of the spirits they had met there. They also disclosed wisdom these spirits had bestowed upon them.

Such carvings & wisdom rarely deviated from set forms. Minor bits of creativity might be added, but the masks remained to the highest degree conventional, not only within a single village, but over great spans in time & space.

In short, when the task of artistic inspiration & creation was assigned to the unconscious, the images that resulted were corporate ones. They didn't come out of the depths of any private unconscious. The dreamer looked inward, but his dream took him directly to an ancient storehouse of tribal experience. What he learned there equipped him to handle functions of the mind too obscure for deliberate, conscious activity, and to do so with ease, communicating with others who shared these complex memories & perceptions.

A Canadian artist recently went on CBC radio to ask listeners to let him borrow old home movies. He assembled these into a remarkable document—remarkable because it enables us to perceive, with some objectivity, our clichés, our collective unconscious, something otherwise so immediate, so obvious, we can't step back from it.

When Hollywood films were films, they were lived; as late TV shows, they can be studied, seen for what they are: part of our collective unconscious. As advertising changes, it reveals itself as folklore. A manual for would-be writers, entitled *Plots That Sell to Top-paying Magazines* (1952), offered a breakdown of magazine short story themes. Specific magazines, it said, accepted only specific themes & published these over & over with only slight variations. To save time in determining these themes, it advised readers to skip the stories & look at the ads: "The key is in the ads."

DÉJÀ VU

When students in California told me of reliving experiences from earlier times, I dismissed their stories as just more of the California scene. But when I heard similar accounts from Ann Arbor & New York, I began to seek a rational explanation, not for the experiences claimed, but for claims of such experiences.

I believe television is the answer.

Anyone who watches Humphrey Bogart on the late show go through customs in Hong Kong, may, years later, if he himself actually goes through customs in Hong Kong, feel he is reliving the past.

This feeling will be all the more mysterious if he doesn't recall the film, and who, in fact, consciously recalls more than a fraction of what he sees on TV?

We may not even recall, when seeing a film for the second time, having seen it before. Instead, we are left with the curious sensation of knowing the outcome but not knowing how we know it.

Yet, no matter how vaguely recalled, parts of these experiences are stored in memory. Like dreams, they sometimes resurface.

Television extends the dream world. Its content is generally the stuff of dreams & its format is pure dream.

Consider an experiment run by Dr. Herbert Krugman, psychologist at General Electric. A subject, with tiny electrodes fixed to the back of her head, was comfortably seated before a simulated TV set. She was told to relax & look at a magazine until commercials came on the screen.

Three commercials were shown, each three times. One was quiet, with pleasant outdoor scenes. The second was also very gentle. But the third was explosive, showing fastballs hurled at an unbreakable sheet of plastic.

Fast brain waves, produced in response to the magazine, indicated relaxed attention, interest & mental activity. Slow brain waves, produced in response to the TV commercials, indicated a relaxed condition with elements of both drowsiness & alertness. This characteristic mode of response to TV developed within 30 seconds, didn't change significantly between soothing & exciting commercials, and dropped only slightly with repetition of the commercials.

Reading is hard work. It makes enormous demands upon the neurological system. It employs one sense only, and that sense in a most peculiar way.

Some years ago, it was alleged—first in a medical volume, later in a psychiatric journal—that Africans needed more sleep when taught to read, and that clothes aided them in reading by conserving body heat & energy. Convincing evidence wasn't offered then & hasn't been offered since, but I've gradually come to wonder, on the basis of scattered observations, if that theory may not have considerable merit. I'm not prepared to dismiss out of hand the observation that it's easier for a naked man to watch TV than it is for him to read.

When food was rationed in France during World War II, the largest portions went to those engaged in arduous physical labor & those whose work involved reading & writing.

We think of exhaustion in terms of toil & sweat, but reading, by employing one sense only—sight—and employing it in a highly restricted way, destroys the harmonic orchestration of all the senses. Reading can be more exhausting than physical labor.

Moreover, reading involves language and all languages are highly abstract, their grammars closer to mathematics than to daily sensory experience. And words neither sound nor look like the things they represent. That association must be learned.

The word "house" doesn't look like a house, but a picture of a house often does. Anthropologists like to point out that people who are unfamiliar with photographs must first be taught how to "read" them. This is true, but it's also true that they learn very quickly. There's an enormous difference between reading the word "house" and seeing a picture of a house. Reading makes different demands on the brain.

Media are really environments, with all the effects geographers & biologists associate with environments. We live inside our media. We are their content. TV images come at us so fast, in such profusion, they engulf us, tattoo us. We're immersed. It's like skin diving. We're surrounded & whatever surrounds, involves. TV doesn't just wash over us & then "go out of mind." It goes into mind, deep into mind. The subconscious is a world in which we store everything, not something, and TV extends the subconscious.

Such experiences are difficult to describe in words. Like dreams or sports, they evade verbal classification.

Asked where he has been, a child who has been running, shouting, slipping in the mud, smelling autumn leaves, eating hot dogs, replies, "Out." Asked what he has been doing, he says, "Nothing." Finally the parent extracts an acceptable answer: "Playing baseball." But that reply is adequate only to the parent. The child knows how inadequate words are for any total sensory experience.

Any picture is a mass of information in a flash. A written caption or narration may classify bits of this information, telling us what to look at & how to respond to it. But most information on TV is unclassified—like a telephone directory that hasn't been alphabetized.

63

This makes it splendidly attractive to artists & others who seek to create their own worlds. But for most people it means a-never-to-end-too-much-of-things.

Teachers, of course, teach classified information. This is why they love lectures & texts. Any language is itself a great classifier. It makes the complex coherent, the ambiguous explicit. Words show us the difference between "trees" & "bushes," a distinction less clear in life than in language (unless a gardener, with clippers, makes nature resemble language).

Information packaged in words is easier to learn, recall, and have opinions about than information packaged in pictures, especially moving pictures.

How much more difficult to recall unclassified information! How impossible to have opinions about it!

We don't remember very early childhood experiences because they are not encoded in language or any other cultural code.

TV has little to do with communications in the old sense of transfer of knowledge from knower to nonknower. For one thing, there's nobody out there waiting to receive messages, no audience to be bombarded. There are only potential participants.

This is especially true in the modern classroom. Once students were empty buckets waiting to be filled. Now these buckets are overflowing with information acquired outside the classroom. In a world of media crop-dusting, the classroom has become a fallout shelter. It's now a place of detention, not attention.

Unlike print, TV doesn't transport bits of classified information. Instead it transports the viewer. It takes his spirit on a trip, an instant trip. On live shows, it takes his spirit to real events in progress.

But here a contradiction occurs: though TV may make the viewer's spirit an actual witness to the spectacle of life, he cannot live with this. If he sees a criminal making ready to murder a sleeping woman & can't interfere, can't warn

64

her, he suffers & is afflicted because his being is phantasmal.

So he participates solely as dreamer, in no way responsible for events that occur. All TV becomes dream.

This is the inner trip, the inward quest, the search for meaning beyond the world of daily appearances. It's the prophet "blinded so that sight is yielded for insight."

TV is actually a *blind* medium. We may think of it as visual, recording a world "out there." But it records a world within. Sight surrenders to insight, and dream replaces outer reality. TV, far from expanding consciousness, repudiates it in favor of the dream.

Jacques Lusseyran, blinded at the age of eight, tells how he wanted to use his eyes & looked in the direction where he was accustomed to see, but met only with despair. Then, suddenly, he realized he was looking the wrong way. Instead of clinging to the movement of sight toward the world outside, he looked from an inner place to one further within: "Immediately the substance of the universe grew together, redefined and peopled itself anew. I was aware of a radiance emanating from a place I knew nothing about, a place which might as well have been outside me as within. But radiance was there, or, to put it more precisely, light. It was a fact, for light was there."

Like Lusseyran, we've all been looking the wrong way and at first have seen nothing. We judge TV as if it were a modified form of print and, of course, find it wanting. What we overlook is the reality it reveals.

TV is the psychic leap of our time. It's a trip far more potent than LSD. It turns thoughts inward, revealing new, unsuspected realities. Those who prefer this inner reality live in a world apart. A confidential study (network financed) reveals that children west of the Rockies, from 11 to 12 on, are turning off TV, but their parents stick with it, becoming stoned in the process. Drugs, by comparison, are kids' stuff. It's really the silent majority over 30, that gets stoned nightly.

For TV addicts, reality seems messy, stale. They find

daily life heartlessly indifferent to the needs of their imaginative life.

It is sometimes said that natives confuse dreams with reality. They don't, in fact, but the point is that dreams, for them, often constitute a focus for their emotions more substantial than reality itself.

TV is not *wholly* divorced from external reality. Those who visit this inner world sometimes acquire interesting information. They respond emotionally at the outset of a new situation, believing they know in advance what that situation holds. They say, "Oh, I've seen that before," or simply, "Yes, I know."

I once saw some children who, in real life, had never ridden horses before, mount & ride off as if they had done this all of their lives—which, of course, they had, on TV.

On July 31, 1971, the *New York Times* reported a hurricane in southern New York: "John McDonough, who is 17 years old, was in his parents' home in Mahopac Point when the storm passed. 'The trees were blowing right down to the ground,' he said. 'We went down into the cellar. Man it was just like something on TV.' In describing the event, a number of youths used the television simile."

Not everyone finds it easy to reconcile real & unreal worlds. The psychic dislocations of interplanetary travel proved too demanding for some TV viewers. Alan Dundes, the folklorist, reports that TV coverage of the moon landing pushed certain neurotics into overt psychosis.

Media Log

I first went on a museum expedition in 1935 when I was 13. Since then, much of my life has been spent in areas remote from Western centers. I no longer have a permanent home & it's been years since I felt fully at ease in my own culture. I'm happiest when approaching a strange village.

My research is generally very restricted in subject, but often I scribble incidental observations on the backs of envelopes. Most of these never survive, but a few show up from time to time in the bottom of a pocket, like foreign coins left over from forgotten trips.

In glancing through these notes recently, I found the observations superficial, the comments petty. But I decided to include a number of them here because they refer to events which anthropologists rarely acknowledge. I'm reminded of Lyndon Johnson's reply to those who found him wanting: "I'm the only president you've got."

Anthropology covers a wide field, but with a restricted view. Real people & real events often get overlooked. The Mickey Mouse *katchina* shown in this book is an authentic Zuni specimen, circa 1950, but was not collected by an anthropologist or preserved by a museum. It was recognized & preserved by the surrealist artist William Copley.

The notes that follow belong to the world of surrealism where events are experienced from within, not observed from without.

69

In small towns, professional clerks sit before open windows, reading & writing. I noticed one who was plugging his ears with his fingers while he read aloud. I was told this was done at the request of the listener who didn't want to share his letter with the reader.

An 18th century missionary in California sent loaves of bread to a colleague, along with a note stating their number. The native messenger ate part of the bread & his theft was consequently discovered. Another time, when the same messenger was sent with four loaves, he ate two, but hid the accompanying letter under a stone while he was thus engaged, believing his conduct would not be revealed this time, as the letter hadn't seen him eating the loaves.

Sarawak, Borneo;
1957

The shores of the Rejang, near its mouth, are scarcely visible & when approached, unpromising: boring mangrove swamps with Malay houses perched high above the waters & Nipah palms, tall & slender, their 40-foot fronds arching out from their bases. Gradually the muddy river narrows, the trees become taller—some reaching 150 feet, casting shadows —the water becomes cooler, mountain-clear, and the dripping, tree-fern jungle draws closer, until soon we are beneath it, fighting our dugout up white rapids in mountain country.

Each night I sleep in a different longhouse, its veranda dark, smoky, hung with skulls; its interior rooms decorated with brass gongs & great Chinese jars, fiercely beautiful by candlelight.

Today the Penghulus, the longhouse chiefs, have assembled in splendor. Tattooed & armed, in leopard jackets & feathered headdresses, they sit facing Temonggong Jugah, chief of chiefs, who paces back & forth in front of them, pointing at me, then sneering at them: "You with your tattooed fingers [for heads taken]: his hands are clean. You with your spears; he has come to collect them to show to children. You with your parangs [swords]: he is unarmed; he mocks you. Why? *He reads.* He has come so far in a day, you could not travel it in a lifetime. You will not disobey me: your children will come out of the fields and go to school."

Here's a man who recognizes that power today lies in media, not weapons.

Bau, Indonesia;
1957

This is such an insignificant village that for a moment as I approached, I considered sleeping along the trail. Drab pandanus houses, shaded by jungle, encircle a sun-baked clearing. In its center is a one-room school, a tiny cabin for the teacher & a palm sapling that may someday offer shade. The young teacher has one book only: *Geological Strata of York County, Pennsylvania.* But he understands what a book is, what it means to capture words & suspend time; what it means to organize all perceptions & experiences using the format of the book as model. This seemingly irrelevant book, donated thoughtlessly to some mission, couldn't be more appropriate, for it tells him that the true mapping of the universe begins below the surface & that for scientists, truth lies in the underlying structures (laws) which govern appearances.

71

Dislodged from his own culture & unhoused in any single medium, my host is able to perceive literacy with a clarity denied those who live within its assumptions.

He unrolls a mat for me to sleep on but, just as we lie down, voices approach & soon the room is crowded, with other faces peering in from outside, the whole scene illuminated dimly by candles on the floor. Silence. Finally, in a low voice, an old man asks how their children can acquire knowledge unknown even to the elders.

It took only one Niels Bohr to turn Copenhagen into a world center for research in physics: a handful of these village teachers may pull off literacy's revolution here.

Obeimi, Papua; 1971

William James tells of Africans gathering wonderingly round an early traveler who, in the interior, had chanced upon a copy of the *New York Commercial Advertiser* & was devouring it column by column. When he got through, they offered to buy this mysterious object, and being asked for what they wanted it, replied, "For eye medicine"—this being their interpretation of the protracted bath he had given his eyes upon its surface.

I've never overheard illiterates talking among themselves about literacy, but I wish I had. Even those who don't understand the nature of writing are often fascinated by penmanship. The Iban of Borneo & the Eskimo of Baffinland regularly crowded round me when I took notes. Many possessed extraordinary dexterity with knives & drills, yet were so clumsy with borrowed paper & pencil, even they laughed at the results.

However, I think most illiterates grasp the nature of writing very quickly. A few may even understand it almost immediately. There is evidence of incipient writing among technologically primitive peoples, but that evidence always seems to postdate some exposure to literacy, however brief. The singing boards of Easter Island were all collected after Europeans had repeatedly visited the island. This script was observed for the first time by Westerners 94 years after the chiefs of the island had witnessed the Spaniards read a proclamation of annexation, to which the chiefs also affixed their "signatures." These signatures are either simple markings, or representations of birds, or of the vulva, such as occur abundantly among local petroglyphs, and appear unrelated to the script. European contact seems to have been the stimulus to the creation of this remarkable script by these Polynesian chiefs or priests.

The Dogon zodiacal system, an enormously complicated African system that has long fascinated anthropologists, makes more sense when one realizes that the Dogon live close to the Islamic center of Mopti & within 150 miles of the medieval "University" of Sankore. Some claim descent from the Mande, transmitters of Islamic learning, including complicated compendia of magical squares, charms, etc., compiled by Al-Buni & others in the 14th century.

Pictorial mnemonic devices, some of them elaborate & ingenious, are far from unknown in technologically simple societies. But phonetic & syllabic alphabets, independently developed, are known only for the city states, and even the conditions of the city state are no guarantee of such inventions. Men who have never been taught to read, but who have seen someone else reading or writing and have understood that speech can be rendered visually, sometimes combine this understanding with local mnemonic devices.

This is one of the most fascinating features of New Guinea life today. In remote areas, one encounters men who, after only the most fleeting exposure to writing, develop their own systems. They proudly exhibit such efforts, with others crowding around, their faces eager. Strange notes are sent to patrol officers & missionaries or left for them in villages. Scraps of paper with markings on them are hidden in sacred bags along with amulets & other treasures.

These writings range from sophisticated syllabic systems to nonrepeated markings, translatable only by their authors. I doubt if any of these innovations will leave much mark, but for one brief moment they provide glimpses into the minds of men moving almost unaided from speech to writing.

Angoram, New Guinea;
1969

Angoram is a chapter out of Somerset Maugham or Evelyn Waugh, the Yoknapatawpha County of Melanesia, belonging to the past, but intensely alive, full of color & characters, all gathered nightly in the Angoram Club, playing billiards under the Queen's portrait (flanked by dartboard & crossed spears) or relaxing in broken furniture left over from World War II: crocodile hunters, gold prospectors, missionaries, adventurers, traders, remittance men, all drinkers & most smugglers, full of false dreams of the past & baseless hopes for the future, each sustained by some private dream of riches without labor. Such towns need their gold rush or illicit diamond trade: in the Sepik, it's primitive art. Looting the Amboin caves of archeological treasures netted big money, and while little of this reached the looters, it put the smell of treasure in the air, bringing the town to life, corrupting officials & missionaries alike, creating an atmosphere of intrigue & wealth & great conversations.

The Angoram Club's volunteer bartender is a sensitive, witty Australian builder who, having failed at both architecture & suicide, abandoned his past to become the government carpenter in this remote outpost. His thirst for the printed word had reduced him to reading can labels, equipment instructions, even currency, until he discovered a set of the collected works of Aquinas, abandoned by a mad-missionary-turned-dealed-in-pagan-art. Late conversations usually end on some fine Thomistic point.

There were five igloos at Kicertakjuk, each with several "rooms." To enter Amaslak's, you went first through a "hallway," off of which opened three rooms, each with a sleeping platform of snow & a stone lamp burning seal oil. Amaslak, his wife, two children & I had one room; to the left lived his parents & their favorite grandchild; to the right, his sister, her husband & child.

Amaslak was a first-rate hunter. Every moment the weather permitted, sometimes for thirty hours at a stretch, we hunted seal at their breathing holes or along ice cracks or at the floe edge, waiting, waiting, then hitting one, racing out in a kayak to harpoon it before it sank & sometimes eating the meat while it was still warm.

The life of the hunter is a constant adventure. He realizes this & admits it & this element of the lottery attaches him to his calling. In the long run he's always poor, but a tremendous catch makes him rich for a day—opulence unsoured by satiety!

One day we killed a walrus & 32 seal. One seal, captured live, was tortured before being killed. That same day a hunter fell through the ice, but we hauled him out & each donated a piece of dry clothing.

With the returning sun, seal appeared on top of the ice

& we concentrated on killing them. By this time, overland travel was difficult, the igloo intolerably damp, our food supply at its lowest & nearly everyone had a cold.

Toward the end of May, when the sun once more circled the horizon day & night, the snow melted on the ridge tops & sealskin tents were erected. Out of the igloos at last! It was still cold outside & inside, too, but after months of igloo life this was forgotten. The children put up a play tent & brewed tea over a tiny stone lamp. The wooden door to their parents' tent went Bang! Bang! as the children ran in & out—those going out meeting those coming in, the tide turning & all coming in, standing there for a moment, then all rushing out; the same runny nose here, gone, then back.

With the lengthening days, birds arrived from the south & their cries filled the air. The snow gradually vanished. Swiftly, miraculously, flowers appeared & the long arctic winter was over.

Amaslak & I set out for Jens Munck Island where we lived in a small camp & hunted with new friends. From there we moved to tiny Kaersuk Island with its twin peaks from which it takes its name. Six people had wintered there. They formed a classic Eskimo family: husband & wife, his mother, their son, daughter & son-in-law. The girl was exceptionally beautiful. Her husband looked like one of Genghis Khan's lieutenants. The old grandmother, her face covered with purple tattoos, put my finger in her mouth to show me how her teeth wobbled. She called her grandson "Not," her pronunciation of Knud, after Knud Rasmussen, the Danish explorer who visited her over thirty years ago. It was the greatest compliment she could pay, for the Eskimo believe in reincarnation, & thought Rasmussen was once more among them.

Then up Jorgensen Fiord, but already the ice was bad & one day Amaslak insisted we turn back. We raced south, toward the middle of the Melville coast, traveling day & night, sleeping a few hours, then on through the barrier ice—a maze of canyons & hills, some rising thirty feet, colored white & silver & turquoise—leaping cracks, throwing dogs over, shooting seal & frightening walrus into open water, all the time pursued by the sun that melted & cracked the narrow highway we followed along the coast.

Flocks of birds swooped down to look us over, often coming up suddenly from behind, without warning. The sled crashed down an ice slope, skidded close to the dark, open water below, then bridged a great crack, the whip constantly exploding & the two of us racing to keep up, leaping from foothold to foothold, marveling that our legs didn't fail.

We replaced three dogs at camps where we ate, cutting chunks of caribou or seal from meat piled just inside each tent—simply taking it, for Eskimos don't offend by offering.

The route back took us past the Hudson's Bay Company post at Igloolik where I stopped to say goodbye to the Scottish trader. He urged me to choose a book from his shelves, for he said the ice on Fury and Hecla Strait was flat, the day calm, the dogs familiar with the trail & there would be nothing to do but sleep or read.

While the dogs pulled & Amaslak dozed, I read Richard Henry Dana's *Two Years Before the Mast*. I was completely overwhelmed by the experience. For months I had read nothing. Now print transported me to another ocean, another century, offering experiences which seemed, at that moment, more real, more vivid, than those surrounding me. No book ever before affected me so strongly. I was returning to literacy after a long absence, but I wonder: does print have this same power over those who first encounter it? And in postliteracy; can it be that what really troubles us is not the absence of the experience of print, but the experience of the absence of print?

Hollywood, California;
1963

In *I Was a Savage*, Prince Modupe tells of his childhood in French Guinea. He describes how his father, "a mahogany tree of a man," returned from trading on the Niger, exhausted, muddy, smelling of spices & hides, and telling of river adventures.

At mission school, Modupe was so impressed by a map of the Niger he determined to take one back to his village as a gift for his father:

> My father thought the whole idea was absurd. He refused to identify the stream he had crossed at Bomako, where it is no deeper, he said, than a man is high, with the great wide-spread waters of the vast Niger delta. Distances as measured in miles had no meaning for him. . . . Maps are liars, he told me briefly. From his tone of voice I could tell that I had offended him in some way not known to me at the time. The things that hurt one do not show on a map. The truth of a place is in the joy and hurt that come from it. I had best not put my trust in anything as inadequate as a map, he counseled. . . . I understand now, although I did not at the time, that my airy and easy sweep of map-traced staggering distances belittled the journeys he had measured in tired feet. With my big map-talk, I had effaced the magnitue of his cargo-laden heat-weighted treks.

At school, Modupe learned to read: "The one crowded space in Father Perry's house was his bookshelves. I gradually came to understand that the marks on the pages were *trapped words.* Anyone could learn to decipher the symbols and turn the trapped words loose again into speech. The ink of the print trapped the thoughts; they could no more get away than a *doomboo* could get out of a pit. When the full realization of what this meant flooded over me, I experienced the same thrill and amazement as when I had my first glimpse of the bright lights of Konakry. I shivered with the intensity of my desire to learn to do this wondrous thing myself."

Modupe left Africa for the United States where he studied

anthropology, then worked for MGM as an actor & consultant. To avoid offending African governments, MGM insisted that no film on Africa resemble Africa. Modupe's task was purely creative: design buildings, songs, shields, dances, masks, even "languages," all of which Americans would accept as authentically African but which no African would recognize as his. Modupe was so successful in this that he convinced even Africans & they modified their art accordingly.

Modupe often phones me late at night when one of his old films is showing on TV. We watch on our separate screens while he provides a running background. Tribes, he tells me, were generally named after directors by adding vowels to their last names. Hair styles, while not authentically African, were real hair. Extras protested that long hair prevented them from dating girls. Their demands for additional pay were ignored until they began wearing, in the cafeteria, large rubber lips made by the prop department.

I urged Modupe to write a second volume, calling it *Now I Am Civilized*, but his interests are elsewhere & though he laughs about making these films, he never laughs at the films.

Southampton Island, Northwest Territories;
1952

While traveling with Ohnainewk, I remarked, as best I could in Eskimo, "The wind is cold." He laughed. "How," he asked, "can the *wind* be cold? You're cold; you're unhappy. But the wind isn't cold or unhappy."

Not until I arrived did Ohnainewk have anyone to talk to about such things. During the winter of 1910, he had learned a little English from the wife of a Mounted Policeman, and though there had been little opportunity to use it in later years, he had not forgotten it. In this he was unique, for though a few Canadian Eskimo had acquired limited English from early whalers, they were never motivated to transmit it to their children or even to retain it.

Our association resulted in superb English on his part, limited Eskimo on mine. One oaf at the white settlement, who resented Ohnainewk's "pretensions," gave him a subscription to *Fortune* & the *Wall Street Journal*. If he understood the insult, he ignored it; he was too grateful for reading matter on this exciting new world of power. Between visits we corresponded about everything, including the threat to use atomic bombs in Korea: "This is from an eskimo, the entire world seemingly have worked and found a way to distroy people butt are somewhat behind in finding ways to protect their wives and children from the might of thier own distructive weapons. However if you should come up north with your family I should soon find a plase somewhere north of here and I tell you, we should not starve even if we should fall back on bows and arrows & harpoons not for a long while anyway."

Port Moresby, New Guinea;
1970

A recently published Pidgin-English phrase book, by a Hungarian linguist who used a Hungarian-English phrase book as model, offers Pidgin phrases for: "I would like to meet one of the rabbis"; "Please give me a pair of warm gloves. I need a lined leather pair"; "I like skating"; "What is the rag content of this bond paper?"

For a conversation with a doctor, it recommends: "What is your fee for a house call?" In ordering a conservative suit, it suggests: *Mi laikum kainkain bilas bilong ol tubuna*, which actually means, "I like the kind of decorations worn by the ancestors." In ordering a book for a wife who likes romances, it offers: *Meri bilong mi i laikim ol stori bilong man meri pren wantaim*, which means, "My wife likes stories about men and women sleeping together."

Piano, in Pidgin, is *piano*, not *bikpela bokis biling krai taim yu paitum na kikim en* (the big fellow cries when you kick him) and helicopter is *helicopter*, not *mixmaster bilong Jesus Christ*, though a plausible name for mixmaster might be *helikopter bilong misis* since helicopters are better known in New Guinea than mixmasters.

Whatever its origins, and these are certainly ancient & complex, Pidgin is today the lingua franca of modern New Guinea. Grammatically simple, it's easy to learn, and though its vocabulary is small, new words are easily added.

Pidgin has proved remarkably efficient in business, government & education. It is not, however, without its critics. Expatriates, especially missionaries, recently blamed a Cargo Cult, a nativistic revival movement, on Pidgin. Both press & radio had given much coverage to an eclipse & some expatriates alleged that a poor translation suggested the eclipse would last two months. Dr. Ralph Bulmer checked press & radio releases and found no such error in translation. Those who fear Cargo Cults blame institutions they dislike. Missionaries, favoring English, don't like the Pidgin press.

Pidgin puts a backspin on many words, thus slowing down information transfer & making communication easier to follow: *lakim* (like him) instead of simply *lak* (like); *bikpelo* (big fellow) instead of simply *bik* (big). A few suffixes, used repeatedly, provide loose rhymes & rhythms that also aid in communication.

English-speakers often find Pidgin amusing, perhaps because some of its words have a touch of frontier humor: headman is *bos boi* (boss boy); domestic is *monki masta* (monkey master). American teen-agers would love it.

Rubbing two languages & two cultures together can sometimes release old perceptions. In a Pidgin translation of *Mac-*

beth, Macbeth becomes a Highland chieftain, the witches sorcerers & the English army a punitive patrol. An Australian Broadcasting Corporation news report on fighting in Ulster included the song "The Wearing of the Green," with the explanation, in Pidgin, that green & orange were the emblems of two feuding tribes, that defeated Catholics sought to reclaim land once theirs, etc.—an explanation entirely comprehensible to New Guinea Highlanders.

Ideally, a language is a storage system for the collective experience of the tribe. Every time a speaker plays back that language, he releases a whole charge of ancient perceptions & memories. This involves him in the reality of the whole tribe. Language is a kind of corporate dream: it involves every member of the tribe all of the time in a great echo chamber to which each speaker constantly adds new sound tracks.

Alan Lomax writes: "A musical style is learned as a whole and responded to as a whole . . . the very magic of music lies in the fact that its formal elements can conjure up the total musical experience. . . . I have been in villages where one or two tunes brought forth the satisfaction that dozens of melodies did in another place, or that a symphony produced in a city audience. . . . As soon as the familiar sound pattern is established, he is prepared to laugh, to weep, to dance, to fight, to worship, etc. His heart is opened."

Pidgin offers no such depth. Its words are mostly English, and whatever reflections & resonances these have for English speakers, for Pidgin-speakers they merely designate. This flatness has one advantage, if it can be counted as such: it ignores the past or, in the case of New Guinea, the many pasts stored in 700 languages. This leads to shallowness of expression & thought, and serves to brainwash speakers of their histories. But it may also serve to unite disparate peoples & promote the emergence of a wholly new culture. If such a culture emerges, with Pidgin as its language, Pidgin will become a true language, which is always something more than communication.

Amboin Patrol Post, New Guinea;
1969

Amboin is the dream come true of every English schoolboy. A twenty-one-year-old patrol officer, with bush hat, flag & constabulary armed with rifles & bayonets, administers a neat little village of thatched houses in orderly rows, gardens, flowers & government buildings, including his own thatched house in bachelor disorder (with paperback copy, on the floor, of *How to Avoid Matrimony*) and a large calaboose filled at night with prisoners in red lap-laps, most convicted of "disorderly conduct contrary to Sec. 30(D)" but quite happy with the food & excitement of big city life, which includes a bugler—all this in a lovely mist-filled valley with dazzling birds & butterflies, the nearest European settlement being Angoram, about a hundred miles away, and villagers in the opposite direction using stone axes.

Around midnight, I was awakened by a local sing-sing, complete with traditional drums & two-tone flutes, but the song was "Michael Row Your Boat Ashore, Hallelujah," sung to a very fast beat, echoing throughout the hills & valleys. I suppose children learned it at mission school & taught others, including elders who, even in New Guinea, sometimes prefer to join the young in their experiments rather than sit around the depressing men's houses filled with skulls & bad art.

Wewak, New Guinea;
1969

Setting up a tape recorder here is enough to attract a crowd of teen-agers, each anxious to be recorded. Among the songs just recorded, in addition to a variety of indigenous ones, there is one in English, another in Japanese, a third in German. The first could come from radio, phonograph or school, but the second must date from the time Japanese occupation forces established a public school here, while the German song either survives from before World War I or has been learned more recently from a missionary.

Not one singer understood what he sang, yet each pronounced the words clearly. Local songs were also faithfully rendered, though the language & context were often alien to the singer.

In the past, songs were inseparable parts of sacred ceremonies & dances. They remained the identifiable property of local groups. Radio made them common property. The sacred & obscene now go out over the airwaves stripped of meaning: pure music. The only thing meaningful about them is the relationship of one musical note to another. They achieve the "musical" effects of geometrical abstraction.

To a lesser extent, this same principle applies to the graphic arts: detached from context, stripped of association or feeling, shared by aliens, they become abstract art. "Meaning" is no longer intellectual but sensory, unless, of course, art is clearly representational, in which case the viewer provides his own meaning.

Toronto, Canada;
1952

A friend called to say I was on TV. It turned out to be a rerun from last year's series. I've always found it painful, sometimes impossible, to watch or listen to myself, but I forced myself to do so this time because the whole show seemed so alien. It had nothing to do with the way I feel about myself. It was like reading an article with my name on it which some unknown editor had changed out of all recognition.

While I was watching, the phone rang again. The caller identified himself as a radio ham operator, at that moment on the air with a radio ham in Baffinland. Eskimo friends of mine had traveled to a weather station to talk to me. My conversation with them was made all the more remarkable by the visual background on TV.

As a boy I spent my summers beside a lake in the company of many cousins. Around 1930, an uncle set up a movie camera on a tripod, pointing it through the trees, past the shore, toward a distant island, and filmed a group of us playing. Years later he set up a projector where the tripod had stood so that on the screen we saw exactly what we would have seen had it been daylight, save for one difference: everyone was twenty years older & several were dead.

We live in different communities of time, different personalities of time. The electronic world isn't the tribal world of interpenetrating space & all-contemporaneous time, but one of many times going on at once: the world of Magritte & Ernst.

Postscript: On November 30, 1971, five bandits approached a New York bank. The two lead bandits, with shotguns, blasted out the glass doors. Most of the people inside threw themselves on the floor, where the other bandits sprayed them with automatic weapons, wounding twelve.

"Teller Fannie Pandiella raced to an upstairs ladies' room.

" 'One of the robbers chased me,' she said excitedly. 'But when I ran into the ladies' room he stopped and shouted for me to come out. I didn't, so he went away.' "

New York Post, November 30, 1971

Mingende Catholic Mission, New Guinea;
1969

Over a thousand worshipers came to Mass this Sunday, many decked with feathers & flowers, their faces painted, their bodies covered with clay. A few old men were armed, for display, not defense. One woman nursed a baby on one breast, a puppy on the other. Marvelous singing filled the high, old church with its earth floor & log pews. Men with large shells hanging from their noses had to lift these to take Communion. Between services, several clawing, mud-rolling brawls broke out between jealous women, egged on by whooping spectators, but a calm priest slowly drove an ancient truck into each crowd, breaking up the fights, then returned to perform the next Mass. One man wore a photograph of himself on his forehead, in front of his feathers; friends greeted him by examining his photograph.

Kiev, USSR;
1960

Local papers are full of anecdotes about a party of Ukrainian-born Canadian farmers now revisiting villages where they grew up. Crowds follow them, for they are objects of great curiosity, Rip van Winkles from another age, largely unchanged in speech, manner, even dress, from the time they left here nearly fifty years ago.

Some years ago the Swiss art historian Sigfried Giedion asked me to inquire of the Hopi of Arizona what meaning they attached to "life-lines." Life-line is the term used to describe a picture of an animal with a line drawn from its mouth to its lungs or heart. The Hopi occasionally paint such designs on pots & weave them into baskets, though they do so less frequently than the neighboring Zuni.

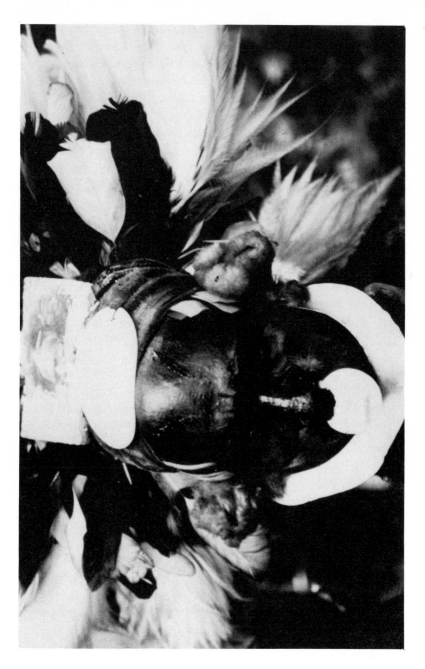

I was staying at Oraibi at the time & one morning I noticed that my hostess was making just such a basket. Her only explanation, however, was that this was how she had been taught. Others overheard the question, but no one volunteered anything, so I let the matter drop.

Later that day I set out across range country with an elderly artist who, though he had traveled widely, remained all Hopi. In his youth, his talents as a traditional Hopi artist led to a scholarship at an eastern art school. But still-life painting didn't interest him & "life classes" embarrassed him. When he returned to Oraibi, fifty years later, the old Hopi art remained within him, largely unchanged. He was more traditional than artists who had never left the reservation.

We climbed a steep mesa, noted for its ancient rock carvings (which women periodically renew by tracing with mud), and sat at the top, looking out over the desert. I knew him well & and spent much time in his company, but this particular conversation, above all others, remains in my memory.

After a long silence, he said, "You asked about the line that goes to the heart. It leads to the spirit which resides in all things—the spirit of life & hope. When we show respect for the spirits around us, they respect us. From this comes good. We show respect in prayer & ceremony—in all things. We demonstrate this by showing that all animals, even snakes, possess souls."

Madang, New Guinea;
1969

My first impression of New Guinea, formed over 25 years ago, was of flies: flies in my eyes, nose, ears, food; flies covering stinking yaws. Great areas of New Guinea still remain isolated & comfortless. But most of the country today has changed so radically that comfort is accepted, even expected.

The Australian National University built transit houses for scientists throughout the Territory, most in towns, some in villages. On the outside, ANU village houses are largely indistinguishable from local houses, but inside, walls are white, showers hot, ice cubes clear.

In publications by anthropologists who stayed in these houses, I found no hint that nearby towns stocked dinner candles, Danish cheeses, German wines, though there were faint suggestions of ordeals suffered in the cause of science.

But even in cosmopolitan Madang there can be problems: the *Post Courier* (October 30, 1969) reports: "CAT ENDED UP IN COOKING POT. A New Guinean has been ordered to pay $5 compensation for eating an anthropologist's cat."

Rocky Brook, Northwest Territories;
1950

One day when Kowanerk & I were alone, she looked up from the boot she was mending to ask, without preamble, "Do we smell?"

"Yes."

"Does the odor offend you?"

"Yes."

She sewed in silence for a while, then said, "You smell & it's offensive to us. We wondered if we smelled & if it offended you."

Tribal life has been described as "a seamless web of relationships" where all information is shared alike by all members. This is certainly true of most information. But not all. Information may be deliberately withheld in playfulness or for power or for many other reasons. Yet my impression is that communications are superb in this tiny igloo settlement. Conversations are tough-minded, yet sensitive. The brutality of life is acknowledged, yet poetry is part of daily living & there is great sensitivity in personal relations.

Life at the government weather station some twenty miles east is quite different. Most of the men there haven't spoken to each other for months. They never leave the base. The jukebox has nothing but outdated popular songs. The library contains 1,500 books, but most are unreadable. One is entitled *English Pewter Marks*. The film library includes "How to Clean the M-1 Rifle," "Venereal Disease" & "Security." This last film has a brief scene with a female spy—a scene the men project over & over, running it forward, backward, upside down, shouting out the same loutish comments, addressed to no one. There is virtually no human communication in this multimillion dollar electronic communications center. There have been several murders at other weather stations this year; there could easily be one here.

New York City;
1972

Twenty-five years ago, the librarian in a museum where I worked, who had run out of shelf space, asked the staff it they would mind keeping the library's reference sets in their offices. After the senior anthropologists had carefully selected what they wanted, I was left with Edward Curtis' forty-volume set of photographs and notes on the American Indian. I was not pleased.

Time has been more generous. In the last few years, a wide audience has discovered Curtis. His major work has been reissued. His photographs illustrate several new books. Three galleries in New York showed his work this year. At least six new collections of his photographs are now in print or on press. A biography is announced.

Anthropologists, who once' dismissed his work as mere romanticism, now find that his account of Kwakiutl ceremonies is actually quite accurate. Moreover, many of his photographs contain valuable details.

But the photographs themselves just don't ring true. Curtis built sets. He supplied wigs. Subjects weren't posed so much as staged, and though the costumes were accurate, the staging was false. A film he made on Kwakiutl life, as he imagined it was lived prior to European contact, though rich in detail, was embarrassingly theatrical, even for 1914.

Curtis was dedicated to an image of an Indian who existed only in romantic literature, and when he couldn't find the Indian in real life, he invented him.

It's an old story. When Queen Anne received four Iroquois sachems—"The Four Kings of Canada"—the resulting publicity told more of London's fashions and fads than of Indians. Contemporary illustrations showed men whose countenance and posture resembled English gentry, even Roman senators, not woodland hunters. Only in minor details e.g., painted body designs, did accuracy prevail.

Voltaire's "Sincere Huron" was Huron only in name. That whole genre of letters, allegedly written by Huron, Chinese, and Persian expatriates in Paris, but actually written by French revolutionaries, was simply a disguised attack on the French establishment. Printers, to mislead censors, sometimes predated and misidentified books, e.g., "Amsterdam, 1771," instead of the correct "Paris, 1779." Ethnologists find little in these books, though they must be a goldmine to political historians.

I cannot find Indians anywhere in the great mass of recent books on them. One book, subtitled "Self-told," consists exclusively of quotations from Indians complaining to white men of injustices. Indians are never quoted talking to Indians. The only identity they are permitted comes from their response to white men.

The popularity of *Bury My Heart at Wounded Knee* didn't derive from any interest in Indians, but from concern over My Lai, over genocide, but genocide hidden in the safe past.

Behind the mask of "Noble Savage" or "Victim as Hero," Indians are simply exploited, their identities stolen from them like land and furs. Their new identities are neither believable nor admirable. Who takes seriously a Noble Savage? Who admires a victim?

Today's Indian exploiters say they write in opposition to genocide. But one cause of genocide is the absence of self-respect based on respect for the identity and integrity of others.

We honor Indian life for that life itself, not for its destruction. It needs no retouching.

Authentic records exist. Perhaps there's no such thing as a true native autobiography, self-told, since preliterates don't write. But there are certainly authentic accounts preserved by Rasmussen, Speck, Emmons, Harrington, Stevenson, Swanton, and others who dedicated themselves to placing on record the meaning of life to native Americans. This handful of strange, rare men, living between two cultures, at home in both but happiest in between, left records of extraordinary beauty and intensity.

The photographic record is also rich. Archives contain vast quantities of early pictures. One Canadian anthropologist recently assembled over 10,000 taken before 1900, on Haida villages alone. Postcard photographers, missionaries, and geologists rarely "staged" shots. They preferred to record real people being themselves.

Robert Flaherty's portraits of Eskimos and Indians were made before 1914, when he was a mining engineer: they are magnificent, but alas unknown. Flaherty was to Curtis what Cartier-Bresson is to a passport photographer.

Why, then, the interest in Curtis? For one thing, his pictures are easy to look at. They have about them a soft, slack romanticism which, like nostalgia, is now in fashion.

They are also readily available and require little research, which means they are ready-made for quick publishing rip-offs.

Though I have written, over a period of fifteen years, on a variety of topics concerning my life with the Eskimo, I have not, until recently, attempted to describe those experiences that touched me most, the images that come to mind when I think back, the ones I live with. I've wondered whether this failure derived from personal censorship or from poverty of expression; whether the words used to cover ordinary experiences failed when the situation went beyond; whether the spirit & memory didn't recede as well. The few times I tried, in relaxed moments, to tell someone what it felt like to undergo intense happenings, I faltered: "It was more involved than that . . . I guess I loved her, but that says nothing . . . he sat in the dark, crying, blaming me. . . . " Words failed, images failed, even memory failed. The whole key & rhythm of my life had been altered forever by a handful of experiences that left no communicable mark. And even now, as I wait for the right words, I wonder how accurate, how honest, these descriptions will be, and to what extent I am working them up a little afterward.

For months after I first arrived among the Aivilik, I felt empty, clumsy, I never knew what to do, even where to sit or stand. I was awkward in a busy world, as helpless as a child, yet a grown man. I felt like a mental defective. There was so much distance between us, such unnatural silences. So I smiled a lot, though smiles come grudgingly to me, and helped lift, pull, or do anything. These efforts were met with stares. But gradually my feelings of stupidity

93

& clumsiness diminished, not as a consequence of learning skills so much as becoming involved with a family, with individuals. If they hadn't accepted me, I would have remained less than an outsider, less than human.

I had done extended fieldwork before, in the tropics, and did more later. But this was different. I recall an afternoon with an Eskimo whom I admired and his daughter whom I loved. She was betrothed. I was married. He once sent her to me, an act that embarrassed me & hurt her. She was named after his first wife, whose memory I knew he lived with. The sealskin tent was warm & close; all of us were laughing at his stories until she saw her eldest half-brother approaching with his team along the coast-ice & spoke to her father: "Son-ours-comes, betrothed." It was a spontaneous outburst, at once tender, incestuous, pleading, yet with full awareness of its effect on each of us.

Such experiences left me indifferent to the cold reports coming out on the Eskimo: they were alien to all I had experienced. I gradually stopped taking the wrapper off the *American Anthropologist;* I let my membership in that organization drop; I listed my occupation as teacher, not anthropologist.

In the early fifties there was only limited interest in Arctic research & even less backing. So I helped dig the Toronto subway & worked nights in a brewery to finance trips, a breach of faculty etiquette my colleagues never forgave. On the first trip, my food never arrived—a great asset—and soon I abandoned all gear, traveling unencumbered, dependent on hosts. It was still a primitive world. The Iglulik used stone lamps; impoverished Okomuit hunted without cartridges; an angakok publicly hung himself following an unsuccessful séance.

But soon the Canadian Arctic was drawn into the world battleground and anthropologists settled about the posts, exhausting the traders' liquor & misinformation. They seemed uniformly unhappy, counting days until they left. I assumed they would publish nothing, because they experienced nothing, or if they did publish, their reports would be ignored. I was doubly wrong. They published voluminously & they all took one another's publications seriously.

I speak only of Canadian reports, for though I've visited Alaska, Greenland, Siberia & Outer Mongolia, these trips were superficial. Most Canadian reports I judge to be based on casual observation, full of heavy theory, fusty kinship data & pretentious claims to insights into self-concepts, all badly written & few of lasting value. Most are so dull they lessen man's respect for man. I see anthropology as far more than the study & presentation of man. It's experiencing man: sensing, appreciation, recognition. It's art.

We're not all agreed on this, of course, but we are agreed—at least we pay it lip service—on the necessity of accuracy. I checked one voluminous Eskimo kinship study and found a 32 percent error in marriages alone: the investigator simply had not known who was who. In another instance, an Oblate missionary forwarded to me a list of Eskimo kinship terms requested by an itinerant anthropologist; he asked that I locate the man whose name he had forgotten. The list, to which the missionary had been asked to add the Eskimo equivalents, had been copied from *Notes and Queries on Anthropology*—a childlike manual on how to do fieldwork.

When I encountered these same anthropologists at conventions, they didn't seem at all ludicrous. They were poised, sure, condescending. Their data & theories seemed eminently suitable to their role as government advisers. They communicated easily among themselves, reaffirming concepts that arose solely from professionalism, unencumbered by those thrilling insights that pierce the hearts of those who care nothing for professionalism.

Shallow fieldwork & bad writing are forgiven on the assumption that if a professional was "there," his data must be valuable. "Being there" is regarded as necessary & sufficient. Civil War veterans who read *The Red Badge of Courage* said, "Crane must have been there. No one else could have known what it was like." Yet we know he was born six years after Appomattox and, at the time he wrote, had never seen a battle. The details he heard from veterans; the truth of terror he learned by more complex means. *Top of the World* contains superb Eskimo dialogue, yet its author, Hans Ruesch, never saw an Eskimo. Knud Rasmussen & Peter Freuchen combined fieldwork with genius; the world knows the Eskimo through their books, not because they were the first to publish, which they weren't, but because they experienced man & left us intense, beautiful revelations.

New York City;
1971

Recently a publisher hired me to examine a manuscript for an anthology of Eskimo poems he planned to publish. His poetry editor had gathered the poems rather hastily and there was some uncertainty about just where the poems came from. When I examined the sources, I found most were anthologies and these, in turn, drew from earlier anthologies. The final versions were often three & four generations removed from the originals and, not infrequently, remarkably different from them. Each anthologist had modified the poems to fit his own temperament, above all to fit his audience, until successive editings had eroded all traces of the originals.

Since most people don't know what poetry is, least of all Eskimo poetry, and couldn't recognize it if they saw it, the anthologist's task is clear: give them rhymed sentiments sprinkled with Elizabethan pronouns. This is what they want. This is what they get.

Moroever, make the same thing available in green & yellow. Call it Japanese poetry, Aztec poetry, children's poetry, ghetto poetry, but make it all alike, all part of a single genre, easily digested, familiar & bland. The real thing may stick in the throat, but this goes down without a cough. If an

96

occasional chaser is needed, an introduction will provide that.

The success of Disney's TV series on people & places was based on this formula. Twenty cultures were chosen, scattered among tundra, desert & jungle, but even though the people dressed in different clothes & ate different foods, they were all alike, members of a single culture. That culture was *our* culture—more accurately, our clichéd image of ourselves that might be called the Hallmark greeting card view.

I believe this same criticism applies to the Eskimo films production by Educational Services, Inc., for the American educational system, though this series is on a much higher level. The audience enjoys a painless, undemanding, mirrored image of itself, under the illusion it is experiencing an alien culture. I cannot find Eskimos anywhere in these films. I *can.* find Eskimos in the writing of Rasmussen. But not here. What I see, instead, is the American educational system, its values, its views.

Nor do I believe these films will survive, the way I'm convinced Rasmussen's writings will survive. I am reminded of art forgeries. Often forgeries, at the time they are made, are widely accepted but when fashions change, their fraudulent nature suddenly becomes clear & people wonder how anyone could ever have been misled by such obvious misrepresentations.

They were misled because what they saw was themselves. Oscar Wilde once remarked that "Wordsworth found in stones the sermons he had hidden there," and apparently we are all Wordsworthians at heart.

Consider that best-selling photography book *The Family of Man*. Superb photographs of people from around the world were combined with quotations from great poets to make an overall statement: that there is absolutely no difference between people. Though people differ in color & creed, they all love, quarrel, protect their children, etc., exactly as we do. The message is clear: we should love them because they are like us. But that statement has its questioning brother: what if they aren't like us?

Fortunately, that question never arises, for today as we travel from channel to channel on TV, we like everyone we see, since we see only ourselves. True, it's a rather bland self, but it's available in any color and it is *our* self.

The saddest part of this story is that the subject becomes an eager victim. People who have long been denied public identity, or cast in degrading roles, now rush on stage, costumed according to our whim.

Kiunga, Papua;
1969

NBC sent a film crew into West Irian, just over the border from here, to penetrate beautiful, mysterious Valley X, so isolated its inhabitants have no memory of other humans. In fact, the filmmakers went into an area where some years before they themselves had filmed "The Sky Above, the Mud Below." The area is remote, but hardly unexplored. Moreover, it hasn't escaped the turmoil of West Irian's independence movement. A number of leaders in this movement, pursued by Indonesian troops, tried to escape across the mountain border, and there have been reports—how true, I don't know—of atrocities, including the killing of local villagers.

The filmmakers parachuted in, though they could have walked in or taken one of the available helicopters. Once down, they filmed the villagers' wonder & astonishment at the appearance of strangers with strange gadgets. In fact, the villagers' reaction was mainly one of displeasure—they wanted the filmmakers (and the Indonesian paratroopers accompanying them) to leave.

On their way out, by inflated boats via a mountain river,

they lost everything—equipment, boats, film—save the radio with which they summoned a nearby helicopter. The pilot tells me they plan to replace their equipment & parachute back into beautiful, mysterious Valley X, there to film the wonder & astonishment, etc. (They did.)

All this is good fun until one realizes that some day New Guineans will know their heritage through such films and Americans will know the rest of the world through such fantasies.

We use media to destroy cultures, but we first use media to create a false record of what we are about to destroy.

Igibia, Papua;
1970

This village was visited a few months ago by a Lowell Thomas film crew. When we arrived a few months later, the villagers didn't know at first whether we were census-takers or malaria-control people or what-have-you, but the instant they saw cameras, they rushed about for props, then sat in front of the cameras, one chopping with a stone axe, another finger-painting on bark, a third starting a fire with bamboo—Santa's workshop. They were all Equity actors.

When the Lowell Thomas film was released by NBC, it was announced that Thomas had "found a village whose inhabitants had never before seen a white man." In fact, the film crew went no more than a few hours' walk from the government base camp at Obeimi & the village they filmed contained a government rest-house. Lowell Thomas himself got no farther than subdistrict headquarters at Nomad, where he stayed eighty minutes, arriving after the entire film had been shot, except for scenes of himself. In what was to be the opening shot, he looked out of the window of the plane & began, "We're now flying over the Great Tibetan Plateau. . . ."

"Cut! Sorry Mr. Thomas, it's the Great Papuan Plateau."

When they reached Nomad, the camera was set up for what was to be the final scene. Standing in front of the subdistrict headquarters with Assistant District Commissioner Robin Barclay, Thomas—dressed in cowboy hat & Texas boots—began, "I'm standing here with the Austrian Patrol Officer Ron. . . ."

"Cut! Sorry, Mr. Thomas, but Robin's Australian & he's the ADC."

Thomas began again. "I'm standing here with Robin Barclay. Barclay's tough. Why? No one knows."

"Great, Mr. Thomas, just great! But could we have just one more take. Go slower on the 'Why' and very thoughtfully on the 'No one knows.' "

Thomas adjusted his Stetson & started again: "Barclay's tough. Why?????????? No. one. knows."

When Barclay, an Olympic athlete, now walks into a bar in Daru, some drunk begins, "Barclay's tough. Why??????????" and the others all chorus, "No. one. knows."

There was nothing funny, however, about Lowell Thomas' completed film. The most charitable thing one could say was that it was forgettable. Forgettable to us, that is. But to New Guineans? The power of film is such that they may someday accept this as a valid record of their ancestry.

Mendengo, New Guinea;
1969

Our troubled epoch seeks to discern in the art of savages not only the expression of another world, but also that of those monsters of the sea-depths which psychoanalysis fishes for with subtle net—and politics or war, with dynamite. Like the Chinese or the "noble savage" of the 18th century, our Primitives step forth obligingly, when called from their retreats. But J. J. Rousseau had not the slighest wish to become a Tahitian, or Diderot a Chinese, or Montesquieu a Persian; they merely wished to annex the wonders and wisdom of these exotic creations of their fancy, and invited them to arraign "civilization," not with a view to destroying, but perfecting it.

—André Malraux
Voices of Silence

We have called primitive man forth from his retreat, reclothed him as a Noble Savage, taught him to carve the sort of art we like, & hired him to dance for us at lunch.

This tiny village on the Sepik has been signed up by a travel agency. A chorus line of ancient crones with withered tits & grass skirts, two bald & all bored, shuffle back & forth in front of eleven tourists who sit in aluminum lawn chairs, eating lunch from plastic boxes. One tourist, with pith helmet & safari jacket complete with Explorers' Club insignia, is taking notes. "Aren't you eating?" asks a companion. "No," he replies, "I haven't had a bowel movement in three days." It turns out none of the others have either.

In the world of electronic technology, we humbly encounter the primitive as avant-garde. Americans, Englishmen, Spaniards, Italians, Japanese flock to the Sepik, board palatial houseboats and, drink in hand, solemnly view savages on the hoof. This search for the primitive is surely one of the most remarkable features of our age. It's as if we feared we had carried too far our experiment in rationalism, but wouldn't admit it & so we called forth other cultures in exotic & disguised forms to administer all those experiences suppressed among us. But those we have summoned are generally ill-suited by tradition & temperament to play the role of alter ego for us. So we recast them accordingly, costuming them in the missing parts of our psyches & expecting them to satisfy our secret needs.

Since he was first contacted by the West, primitive man has been forced to serve his conqueror's many needs, not the least of these being aesthetic. In New Guinea, the time element is so condensed that collectors of primitive art can, in comfort, penetrate prehistory, arriving with gin & tonic in hand. Both banks of the Middle Sepik are now lined with workshops where tourist art is turned out en masse. One mission has a huge antiquing area. Posh safari boats with staterooms, bars & showers pass each other on the river, filled with art collectors, psychiatrists, photographers, etc. all anxious to meet Stone Age man face-to-face, collect his art, hear him sing & do all this without discomfort or delay.

Those who can't make the trip aren't denied. This same art is exported to American department stores & museums. One museum displays New Guinea tourist art, but keeps fine authentic pieces in storage. Curators & public, knowing New Guinea through the media, distrust the genuine.

The most popular New Guinea carvings sold in America are crude Maprik figures of nude males with birds on their heads (thus combining primitivism, sex & religion). Figures with erect penises are especially popular. One Los Angeles department store, unable to sell figures with dangling penises, donated them to local universities.

No man can embrace True Art
Until he has Explor'd and cast out False Art.
——Blake

Contrary to much that has been written, stone carvings made by modern Canadian Eskimos do not constitute an indigenous art newly discovered but ancient in origin. These carvings came into being after 1949, as the direct result of the teachings & promotions of James Houston, an artist representing first the Canadian Handicraft Guild & later the Canadian government. The carvings share little with traditional Eskimo art or even with Alaskan or Greenlandic souvenirs, though they do show marked resemblances to Houston's own art work. Full credit goes to him, not for liberating a repressed talent, but for creating a new, delightful art that brings financial assistance to needy Eskimos & joy to many Western art connoisseurs.

Most of these carvings are massive, heavy & fragile, designed to be set in place & viewed by strangers. The traditional role of art is gone: object has replaced art. Traditional prespective is gone: stability & single perspective have replaced mobility & multiple perspective. Traditional notions of discovery & revealing are gone: asked by the Queen how he decided what to carve, an Eskimo replied that he consulted Mr. Houston because he had no desire to produce anything unsalable.

That Eskimos could move into a new art form with ease & success is significant: clearly old resources combined with new notions of individualism. That the government should promote this art is understandable: such publicity increased Eskimo income, helped certain government agencies & policies, and appealed to Canadian nationalism.

What is less commendable is the acceptance of this propaganda as reliable and this art as "Eskimo." To link art with souvenirs seems equally misplaced. "It's the power of belief," writes Froelich Rainey, "which makes all the difference between original native art and contemporary native crafts."

Can the word *Eskimo* legtimately be applied to this modern stone art? I think not. Its roots are Western; so is its audience. Some carvers have been directly trained by Houston; others follow a governmental manual. Carvings are produced by Eskimos working at craft centers in the north and by tubercular Eskimos in southern sanatoriums. Not a few are made by Chinese in Hong Kong, a competition that led the Canadian government to put labels of "authenticity" on Eskimo-made carvings. The following news item shows how complicated even this became:

OTTAWA: Jack Shafter, vice-president of Regal Toy Co., today accused the Department of Northern Affairs of "wheeling and dealing" in making private arrangements for commercial production of Ookpik, the fuzzy, saucer-eyed version of the Arctic owl. Designed by an Eskimo woman in Fort Chimo, N.W.T., and made of sealskin, Ookpik was promoted by the Government at trade fairs. When orders outstripped Eskimo production, Northern Affairs granted rights to the Reliable Toy Co. to manufacture Ookpiks of white plush synthetic fabric to sell at about $2.98. Another version, made of imported possum pelts, sells at around $7. Ookpik has been registered with the trademark division and unauthorized copies are illegal. Lawrence Samuels, vice-president of Reliable, said: "We've been told bluntly to keep our mouths shut about this thing. Any public relations or publicity will have to come from Northern Affairs."

In addition to carving stone, Eskimos were trained to make totem poles, pottery & prints, though all were alien to Eskimo culture. Production of totem poles was abandoned and pots sold poorly, but prints proved enormously popular. They combined Siberian designs with techniques learned directly from Japanese printmakers. By error, Siberian designs were included in a booklet on Canadian native designs and Eskimos were given this booklet for reference. Many Eskimo prints

104

displayed in art museums & printed on Christmas cards owe their forms to this error.

That Eskimo artists have the desire & confidence to improvise is a happy situation. I regret, however, that the new ideas & materials they employ are supplied by us, not selected by them. We let the Eskimos know what we like, then congratulate them on their successful imitations of us.

What shall we call this new art? Eskimo? If so, what does that word mean?

In the United States, many of the plastic Christian art objects are produced by Jews: plastic Jesuses for dashboards; grains of sand from the Red Sea embedded in plastic cubes with the caption: "He trod on this"; even a plastic do-it-yourself crucifixion kit. The fact that Jews make these doesn't mean they are Jewish art. They remain Christian art—made for, used by & believed in solely by Christians.

Eskimo art is made for, used by & believed in solely by Westerners—that is, until recently. Now it also serves to give identity to the Eskimo themselves. Having deprived the Eskimo of his heritage, even memory of this heritage, we offer him a substitute which he eagerly accepts, for no other is permitted. And so he takes his place on stage, side by side with the American Indian whose headdress comes from a mail-order catalogue, who learned his dances at Disneyland & picked up his philosophy from hippies. He knows no other identity, and when he is shown the real treasures of his culture, when he hears the old songs & reads the ancient words, he aggressively says, "It's a lie, a white man's lie. Don't tell me who I am or who my ancestors were. I know."

In cigar stores, art galleries & museum shops across Canada, Eskimo stone art is available, popularly priced, popularly styled. Carvings of mermaids, those sexually frustrating figures from our own mythology, are especially popular. Here they are identified with the Eskimo goddess Sedna, though neither carvers nor buyers can be much concerned with accuracy, for these carvings always show a girl with two eyes, fingers & braided hair, whereas Sedna was one-eyed, fingerless & unkempt.

Of the myths that were once half-told, half-sung in the igloos, none was more important than that of Sedna. Every Eskimo knew it & had his own version, all equally true, for this myth was too complex for any single telling.

Sedna or Nuliajuk ("Young girl") rejected all suitors until a stranger induced her to elope with him. He was, in fact, a cruel dog disguised as a man, but she discovered this only after reaching her new home on a distant island.

Escape was impossible until one day when her family came to visit her. Her husband always refused to let her leave the tent, except to go to the toilet, and even then tied a long cord to her. But this time when she went outside and he called, asking why she delayed so long, she had the ball of cord reply that she would soon return.

In the meantime, she ran to the beach & joined her parents in their boat. But no sooner had they set out to sea, than her husband discovered the ruse and, transforming himself into a bird, swooped low over the fleeing family, turning the sea to storm, and threatening them with drowning. To save themselves, they cast Sedna overboard.

At first she clung to the gunwale. But her father cut off the first joints of her fingers; when she persisted, he cut off the second & third joints. They sank into the sea to become the seal, walrus & whale that the Eskimo hunt today.

In desperation, Sedna hooked her elbows over the side,

but her father struck her with his paddle, gouging out an eye, and she sank into the sea, fingerless & one-eyed.

From the bottom of the sea, she ruled all creatures. Their floating bodies nearly filled her house. Periodically she sent animals forth to be taken by hunters, but only by hunters who showed respect for slain animals.

Other hunters returned empty-handed. That is, Sedna withheld life from them, for they could not survive without the food, clothing & fuel that came from her subjects.

She was the most feared of all spirits, the one who, more than any other, controlled the destinies of men.

In the various versions of this myth, Sedna was sometimes an unwanted daughter cast into the sea by her father, or a girl who has rejected all eligible men, or an orphan nobody wanted; in one version she was already a mother, abandoned by her own children. In each, she was someone the family abandoned for its own safety.

Abandonment of people was not purely mythical. The Eskimo did, in fact, abandon old people. Killing new-born girls was common. And the position of orphans was precarious: one's own family always took precedence. These were normal experiences in Eskimo life—cruel necessities forced on them by scarcity.

The Sedna myth represented this dilemma as the Eskimo saw it. They never asked that the universe be this way. But—*ayornamut* ("it cannot be otherwise")—they accepted life on its own terms.

They did more than accept: they took upon *themselves* the responsibility for the fact that life was the way it was. They gave Sedna the power of life & death over man. Those who were forced to abandon her now placed themselves in her power, dependent upon her good will, her respect for life.

The hunter Aua, asked by the ethnologist Rasmussen to explain why life was as it was, took him outside and, pointing to hunters returning empty-handed after long hours on the ice, himself asked, "Why?" He then took him into a cold igloo where hungry children shivered and into another igloo where a woman, who had always worked hard and helped others, now lay miserably ill. Each time he asked, "Why?" but received no reply.

"You see," said Aua, "you are equally unable to give any reason when we ask why life is as it is. And so it must be. All our customs come from life and turn toward life; we explain nothing, we believe nothing, but in what I have just shown you lies our answer to all you ask."

The last part of the Sedna myth told of a maze to be entered & come out of alive, bringing the innocent to safety. In this maze there lived the dog whose name was Death. It fell to the *angakok*, or shaman, to find the door that opened the past, unravel the tangled traces of time, rescue the innocent & beware the dog. The occasion was a séance where the *angakok* sought to cure the sick & save the dying. If he failed & his patient died, its soul went beneath the sea to Sedna's home. The *angakok* followed, traveling on the sound of his drum. Sedna's husband, a snarling dog, guarded the entrance to her home, but the *angakok* paralyzed him with a chant & entered her strange house, confronting her directly. He tried to reason with her, arguing that she had taken a life without cause. But she ignored him. He begged for pity, but she laughed contemptuously. In anger, he twisted her arm & struck her with a walrus penis bone. But she was not afraid. Then he appealed to her vanity, combing out her tangled hair. But she was still unrelenting. Finally, ignoring her altogether, he stepped back and, with drum held high, sang of life.

Sedna was sometimes so touched by his song, so moved by his singing, she released the soul of the dead person, and the *angakok* returned with it to the land of the living.

In a life where neither reason nor strength prevailed, where cunning counted for little & pity least of all, the Eskimo sang of life, for only that availed, and even that, not always.

A people may be fairly judged by their uses of the past. The myth of the hero who goes to the land of the dead to unravel the threads of time & save the innocent has been shared by many people & woven into their most magical dreams. The ancient Greeks knew the hero as Orpheus. Literate man knew the goddess of the nether world as the Ice Queen in a Hans Christian Andersen fairy tale for children. Modern man knows the goddess as mermaid, debased into a paperweight.

The World Turned Upside Down

When Cornwallis surrendered at Yorktown,
the British lowered their colors,
stacked arms & marched out playing
"The World Turned Upside Down."

SPEAK, THAT I MAY SEE THEE!

New Guinea has been called "the last unknown." Its highest mountains are snow-covered and below these, in early morning, you walk through clouds, your breath visible. Yet tropical swamps lie immediately north & south.

Port Moresby, the capital of the eastern section, resembles a southern California town with air-conditioned buildings, supermarkets & drive-in theater. Four hundred miles to the west, tiny, isolated bands practice cannibalism.

The bulk of the population lies between these extremes, living in thousands of tiny villages & speaking over 700 different languages.

In 1969-70, the Territory of Papua & New Guinea hired me as a communications consultant. They sought advice on the use of radio, film, even television. They wanted to use these media to reach not only townspeople, but those isolated in swamps & mountain valleys & outer islands.

I accepted the assignment because it gave me an unparalleled opportunity to step in & out of 10,000 years of media history, observing, probing, testing. I wanted to observe, for example, what happens when a person—for the first time—sees himself in a mirror, in a photograph, on films; hears his voice; sees his name. Everywhere New Guineans

113

responded alike to these experiences: they ducked their heads & covered their mouths.

When a shy or embarrassed person in our society ducks his head & covers his mouth, we say he is self-conscious. But why does consciousness of self produce *this* response? Does the acute anxiety of sudden self-awareness lead man everywhere to conceal his powers of speech-thought (his breath, his soul) behind the hand, the way an awakened Adam concealed his sexual powers behind a fig leaf?

Could it be that the deeper message these media conveyed wasn't sanitation or Westminster democracy, but self-discovery, self-awareness? Could this in part explain the riots in Rabaul & Kieta, towns where radio was part of daily life? The people of Rabaul had been in close contact with Westerners since 1885, and now suddenly they were marching in the streets.

The Australian administrators were dedicated men, many of them ex-teachers & nearly all from Protestant middle-class backgrounds. They believed in democracy, cleanliness & a personal God, and they promoted these goals via radio. Yet some of those who had listened most attentively to these sermons were now in angry revolt. The administrators were puzzled & asked: what message had really come through?

WHERE THE HAND OF MAN
HAS NEVER SET FOOT

It was important to us to film the reactions of people totally innocent of mirrors, cameras, recorders, etc. Such people exist in New Guinea, though they number only a handful & are disappearing like the morning mist. But, unless it's the interior of Borneo, I know of no other place in the world where such groups exist & even now, within this past year, change may have penetrated everywhere.

To this end, we went among the Biami, an isolated group in the Papuan Plateau. The following excerpts are from government patrol reports:

B. McBride, ADC, Patrol Report, January 19, 1960

On entering BIAMI territory the people proved to be very wary and occasionally openly hostile towards us. These people consistently tried to prevent us proceeding farther east by insisting that neither tracks nor population lay in that direction; these people obviously wanted the patrol out of their territory. On two occasions the patrol was confronted with a considerable body of armed strength. Only six women were seen amongst the BIAMI and these were accidently met in gardens.

Finally at SODUBI, near the GEWA river, the patrol was openly attacked when we tried to continue east to link up with the area reached by Mr. BUTLER in his patrol from

LAKE KUTUBU. An air drop was called for as food supplies were in short supply and we wished to remain in the area. I did not wish to have to resort to taking food from gardens as this would undoubtedly have aggravated the situation.

Patrol Report, Nomad Base-Camp, May 23, 1962

The native situation would leave little to be desired then, if it were not for the continued aloofness of the BIAMI group which from all accounts is the most populous group of the people which we will have to deal with in the future. The Camp was visited by a small party of about a dozen BIAMIs, all warrior types, on the 17th of January, but this has been our only contact with them. We were unable to communicate with them, having no interpreter, but they made no obvious attempt to be friendly; on the contrary, they seemed surly and suspicious. They explored the Camp thoroughly and as I had a considerable distrust of their motives, decided upon a firearms demonstration. They observed it with reasonable indifference and as soon as it became dark, disappeared into the bush. Four days later some GEBUSI men came into the camp at eight o'clock at night and told us in some agitation that the BIAMIs were coming down to attack us. However, though we kept a careful watch for a week, nothing happened. We have heard from local sources that the whole time Mr. McBRIDE was patrolling in the BIAMI, the young men wanted to attack the patrol to gain possession of the axes and knives, but that the older men urged caution against the rifles. This balance of forces resulted in only a sporadic attack on the patrol. I had hoped that this BIAMI business would have resolved itself, that friendly contacts would have been made from the camp here, but in five months there has been only this one brief, unsatisfactory contact with them.

Patrol Report, Nomad, March 1969

Arrest those ADUMARIs involved in attacks on JOHNSON's 1968 patrol; arrest those SABASIGIs involved in killing and cannibal eating of a SOIA village male in early January 1969.

Patrol Report, R. I. Barclay, Nomad, March 20, 1969

Summarized outstanding investigations in the BIAMI:

1/ Murder and cannibalism of the man DINOU of DIBALIBA village. SAI'A and OULI, the two actual murders, are still at large, hiding with the remainder of the group. Mr. DARAS-WELLS was thus unsuccessful in their apprehension.

2/ The two murderers captured for the killing of the men at BABAGULIBI have since escaped from the lock up at NOMAD, and are believed to be at large in the TIGASUBI area. Their apprehension will be attempted on my forthcoming patrol to the ADUMARI commencing the 24th March.

3/ Murder and presumed cannibalism of SAMADORO men in December by the KABASI group.

4/ Murder and presumed cannibalism in November of man from KUNOU area by KABASIs. Mr. YOUNG has investigated 3 and 4 with no results (P/R No. 13, 68/69). I will attempt a further investigation when I patrol the TOMU in about three months.

5/ Arrow wounding at WALIBI, IGIMI of KABLIFI victim. GOGUBAIDON of YASOLU (SAWAEBIA) still at large (see Diary).

6/ The aggressive and threatening attitude of the intractable and truculent ADUMARI towards previous patrols through their area. The forthcoming patrol is designed to deal with this.

Patrol Report, Nomad, March 24, 1969

Two women accused of sorcery were forcibly taken into the bush, bound to trees, and systematically beaten. They were left overnight, the plan being to return to them in the morning, beat them again, execute them with arrows, apportion their bodies and eat them—this being the traditional treatment of sorcerers. However, in the morning the women were released: three of the four men on their own admission said that they would have liked to have killed the women but that they already held a "Government BOOK" in the village and were frightened of what the government might do to them if they did kill the women. Having slept on it, they decided to let them go. . . . On this occasion, government influence through the image of the "Book" no doubt saved the lives of the two

117

women even when the Provisional Village Constable was no longer mindful of his position and obligations.

Patrol Report, Nomad, September 1969

On Monday 21st September, two UNAWOE males came in to report the killing and cannibalism of one of their women by the DUDUGAMOBIs on approximately 17th September. At this time most of the UNAWONI males were absent working on the NOMAD/OBEIMI road.

Briefly, one of the DUDUGAMOBI men, NAUWABO, was taken sick and was near death on the night of Tuesday 16th. The remainder of the DUDUGAMOBI males held a singsing, and one SESEBALI in a trance discovered the name of the sorcerer who had made NAUWABO sick—it was NOLOME. Early in the morning NAUWABO died; the cause of his death cannot be ascertained. Five males WAGINA, BEBEMO, SAUWEA, ALIBO and WOBAU collected their weapons and went into the sago area. The men surrounded the women and moved in on NOLOME. The other women dashed off into the bush screaming. NOLOME screamed and tried to evade her pursuers but she was unsuccessful. BEBEMO held the struggling woman while SAUWEA smashed into her skull with an axe from behind. The five returned to the village and reported the deed. Two men GOGOSIMA and EMA returned to the sago area to carry the body back to the village. En route they cut out the woman's intestines and threw them into the bush. The body was secreted near the village as the village constable SIAGI was known to be against killings. An unknown number of males and females carried the body off into the bush where it was eaten. The remains were then buried on the UNAWOBI track. It would seem that the idea was that the government could inspect the corpse and see that they had not eaten it. We cannot reconcile this type of thinking as yet.

The VC attempted to report the murder but lost heart and returned to the village. GOGOSIMA, in an attempt to avert the impending visit of the government, made sorcery against the government. This consisted in carrying a small stone in a bilum under his left armpit. He took the pebble out in front of the others and gazed at it, saying that the government would not be able to visit the village as the stone would make them forget about the DUDUGAMOBI raid and send them to other villages instead.

One of the murderers had been to DARU. Incident occurred within 3 hrs. walk of NOMAD, in village that had had more contact than any except WALIBI.

In spite of these conflicts, we found Biami company a constant delight, full of love of children, humor, thrust of life. The immediate cause of cannibalism, or at least its rationale, is sorcery, a belief that the victims had harmed others by psychic means. Government policy is to lean steadily on killers, not cruelly, but not letting up until killings stop. Patrols raid villages at dawn, bash heads & take murderers off to prison for six months.

But this persuasion has largely failed & there is always the danger that the bashed might some day think of bashing as a solution to their own problems.

Instead of asking why men killed, I asked why some refrained. I always received the same answer: fear because their names were entered in "The Book" (Census). I recommended that patrol officers make a great ritual of entering a man's name in "The Book," and attach to each name a Polaroid shot of the man, which he would be shown annually, but not allowed to keep.

This worked in medieval England: the Domesday Book was so called, not because it was for taxation, but because it recorded names. When a cop takes down your name, he takes you over.

MIRROR, MIRROR

A few Biami men had scraps of mirrors, about the size of coins, obtained through distant trade, but my impression was that these scraps were too small for image reflection & were treasured simply as light reflectors.

In one village, a patrol searching for stolen salt discovered a mirror carefully wrapped in bark & hidden in a thatched roof. I never learned what role this mirror had played, but I imagine it was interesting, for I saw nothing else in either villages or jungle that provided any means for self-reflection. Neither slate nor metallic surfaces exist and, for reasons I don't understand, rivers in this area fail to provide vertical reflections, though reflections of foliage can be seen at low angles. I doubt if the Biami ever before saw themselves at all clearly.

Certainly their initial reaction to large mirrors suggested this was a wholly new experience for them. They were paralyzed. After their first startled response—covering their mouths & ducking their heads—they stood transfixed, staring at their images, only their stomach muscles betraying great tension. In a matter of days, however, they groomed themselves openly before mirrors.

I suspect this has been a standard reaction throughout

New Guinea as mirrors gradually penetrated this island. Nearly a century ago, the Rev. James Chalmers noted that when the Motumotu on the southern coast first saw their likenesses in a mirror, they thought these reflections were their souls.

The notion that man possesses, in addition to his physical self, a symbolic self is widespread, perhaps universal. A mirror corroborates this. It does more: it reveals that symbolic self *outside* the physical self. The symbolic self is suddenly explicit, public, vulnerable. Man's initial response to this is probably always traumatic.

Added to this, mirrors reverse forward & back: walk toward a mirror, the image moves in the opposite direction. That image, moreover, is greatly reduced. Test this yourself: with a piece of chalk, outline your image on the bathroom mirror.

Mirrors have always been fraught with mystery & fear. We have the story about "Mirror, mirror on the wall," and our folklore warns of werewolves & vampires who, lacking souls, cast no reflections. Mental patients sometimes mutilate themselves while watching their reflections; suicides committed in front of mirrors are far from unknown.

In *Nausea*, Sartre writes: "There is a white hole in the wall, a mirror. It is a trap. I know I am going to let myself be caught in it. I have . . . perhaps it is impossible to understand one's own face. . . . people who live in society have learned how to see themselves in mirrors as they appear to their friends."

When mirrors become a part of daily life, it's easy to forget how frightening self-discovery, self-awareness can be. But even with us, in certain psychiatric cases, mirrors can play a role reminiscent of their role when first encountered. I remember a disturbed friend, obsessed with self-loathing, telling me he thought the electric shaver was man's greatest invention: it had saved him, he said, from the necessity of looking into a mirror for the past eleven years.

In the Congo, mirrors were placed in the chests or stomachs

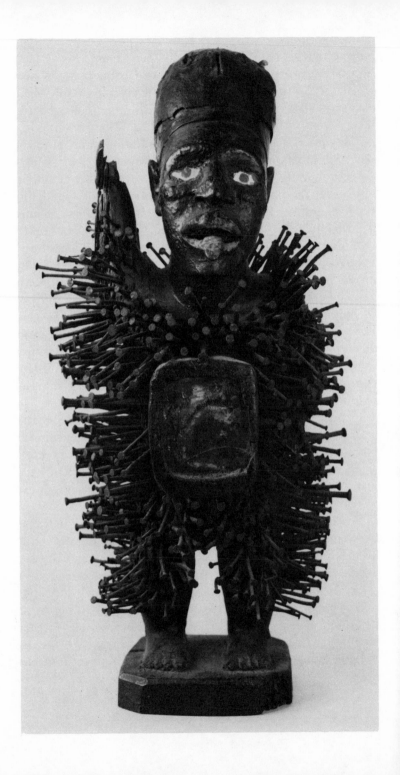

of wooden judicial figures. A defendant would be forced to look into a mirror while nails were driven into the effigy. If he winced, he was judged guilty. In other words, his soul, his identity, entered the statue: he put on that statue.

What made this ordeal so effective, so fraught with fear a guilty man might unwillingly reveal himself, was that it created that intense anxiety which always seems to accompany sudden self-awareness.

SUDDEN SELF-AWARENESS

When people know themselves only from how others respond to them and then for the first time, by means of some new technology, suddenly see themselves clearly, in some totally new way, they are often so frightened, so exhilarated, they cover their mouths & duck their heads.

I think they do so to try to prevent loss of identity. The Highlanders of New Guinea call it loss of spirit or soul, but it's the same phenomenon. It's their response to any sudden embarrassment, to any sudden self-consciousness. When they first see pictures of themselves or hear recordings of their voices, this response is greatly intensified. It's as if they had vomited up an organ; they cover their mouths, almost as a delayed reflex, trying to prevent this loss. In the U.S. Navy, vomiting is called "discovering your soul."

That New Guineans regard the breath as the seat of the soul, and associate speech with intelligence, is understandable. To be conscious is to have breath. What easier way to reveal intelligence than to speak? To be speechless is to be dumb.

Ben Jonson's "Speak, that I may see Thee!" actually comes from the ancient Greeks, who used it as a daily greeting. Like other ancients, they believed breath was the most powerful force radiating from any being. To them, it was the center of life itself.

124

Genesis tells us that when God made man, "He breathed into his nostrils the breath of life, and man became a living soul." To speak meant to call into being: "And God said, 'Let there be light,' and there was light"; "By the word of the Lord were the Heavens made, and all the hosts of them by the breath of His mouth."

Children often identify thinking with the mouth, and thought with the voice. Thought is confused with the thing itself, in the sense that the word is part of the thing. Thoughts are word-things, stored in the breath or chest: the ears & mouth merely receive & transmit them.

> SWISS FATHER: What is thinking really?
> HILDA (4 years, 9 months): Don't know.
> FATHER: Well, what do you think with?
> HILDA: Animals think with their mouths.
> FATHER: And people?
> HILDA: With their tongues.
> FATHER: What does a man do when he thinks?
> HILDA: He speaks.

Among the Trobrianders, intelligence & moral qualities reside in the larynx. In locating it, Trobrianders point to the organs of speech. Memory, that is, traditions learned by heart, lie deeper, in the belly. Power is in words, not things: it resides within man & escapes through his voice.

Society Islanders call thinking "speaking in the stomach" and thoughts "words in the belly." When a sacred recorder (harepo), famous in life for ancient knowledge, is dying, his son & successor places his mouth over the mouth of the dying man to inhale the parting soul: in this way lore is transmitted. Sages attribute their learning to this expedient.

The conception of words as part of the soul—the soul being that which survives death—may lie behind the poet's claim: "Let no man mourn me."

THE FACE OF MINE ENEMY

H. J. Redmond, Patrol Officer, Amboin Patrol Post, October 25, 1962

Found a group of GADIOs on trading expedition to SUMARIUP. They were just as surprised as we, they run into bush parallel to track. Much gesticulating and shouting. Carriers panic slightly and some begin to flee. Police calm them. Self and interpreter go forward and speak with GADIOs. . . . They viewed demonstration of rifle fire with awe. A portable radio transfixed them with utter astonishment. . . . The GADIOs have an astounding appearance. They are fine physical specimens and rather more impressive then the average KARAWARI native. They are fairly tall, lean types. Average height would be about 5'8". Their bodies are heavily muscled and without fat. . . . Typical dress consists of a number of cane hoops fastened around the waist from which are suspended strips of grass and flowers. Their hair is matted and plaited and hangs nearly shoulder length. Most of the men were heavily bearded. On their heads they wear beret/ skull cap like headwear. These caps are made of beaten bark and are held in place by long needles of cassowary bone. On top of these caps are pinned large tree leaves. These leaves (Breadfruit) are dried by the sun. . . . Foot-long cassowary quills pierce the nose and circular bones the ears. Long, thin, curving bones from the tail feathers of the Bird of Paradise also hang along the nostrils. Ropes of girigiri are stretched from ear to ear, across the forehead. Ropes of girigiri and tambu are fastened around the necks and waists. . . . All the men carried beautifully curved and decorated bows and arrows. Some of the carriers tried to purchase a set of arrows but the owners refused to part with them.

Gadio country has since been visited by missionaries & anthropologists. Yet, in several tiny island villages, I sensed a distrust, an unease, I felt nowhere else.

Fear has kept villages isolated, even after tribal warfare stopped. In one valley I stood on a hilltop looking out over a forested valley and asked about a settlement, smoke from which rose in the distance. No one had ever been there. No one knew anyone who had. No one knew a single member of that not-too-distant but once-hostile village. There were only legendary accounts.

When we passed around photographs of these legendary strangers, there was absolute fascination. I saw no evidence of fear. My impression was that in one amazing stroke, fear was reduced & an element of familiarity crept in.

WORLD'S END

We ascended the Wagamush, moving through country so beautiful, past villages so remote, that this living past seemed to deny the very existence of the world from which we came.

As we approached Sio, the village leader stood alone on the bank, confronting us the way Axel Heyst confronted the mysterious trio approaching his remote island in Conrad's *Victory:* their appearance, Heyst felt, was "like those myths current in Polynesia, of amazing strangers, who arrive at an island, gods or demons, bringing good or evil to the innocence of the inhabitants—gifts of unknown things, words never heard before."

We established some sort of rapport by distributing gifts. Then we did nothing. After a few days, women came out of hiding & village life resumed its rhythms.

Sepik villages have had contact with the West since before World War I. Highland villages were drawn abruptly into the world economy during World War II. But those in between remained remarkably untouched. It cost the government money each time it extended its authority & it had no money to waste. A few patrol officers, missionaries, hunters, prospectors, & timber buyers—count them on two hands—moved through these hills, but lightly, leaving little imprint. Some villages escaped even these visits.

Today, Westerners who enter this country make hand-drawn maps of rivers & villages, sharing this information when they meet, for no better maps are available.

What changes occurred came more from awareness of the existence of a world outside, than from direct contact with that world. Tribal hostilities ceased & villages shifted from inland sanctuaries to river sites. At Sio, this relocation was so recent that the old village still stood, its *haus tambaran* sheltering ancient treasures, as well as elders who chose not to move.

Missionaries visit Sio frequently; a local teacher has a handful of students; itinerant traders leave behind steel axes. Yet Sio remains far removed from Western centers. Stone axes were still in use when we arrived; cameras & recorders were absolutely unknown.

We gave each person a Polaroid shot of himself. At first there was no understanding. The photographs were black & white, flat, static, odorless—far removed from any reality they knew. They had to be taught to "read" them. I pointed to a nose in a picture, then touched the real nose, etc. Often one or more boys would intrude into the scene, peering intently from picture to subject, then shout, "It's you!"

Recognition gradually came into the subject's face. And fear. Suddenly he covered his mouth, ducked his head & turned his body away. After this first startled response, often repeated several times, he either stood transfixed, staring at his image, only his stomach muscles betraying tension, or he retreated from the group, pressing his photograph against his chest, showing it to no one, slipping away to study it in solitude.

We recorded this over & over on film, including men retreating to private places, sitting apart, without moving, sometimes for up to twenty minutes, their eyes rarely leaving their portraits.

When we projected movies of their neighbors, there was pandemonium. They recognized the moving images of film much faster than the still images of photographs.

Seeing *themselves* on film was quite a different thing. It required a minor logistic feat to send our negative out, get it processed, then returned, but it was worth the effort.

There was absolute silence as they watched themselves, a silence broken only by whispered identification of faces on the screen.

We recorded these reactions, using infrared light & film. In particular, we recorded the terror of self-awareness that revealed itself in uncontrolled stomach trembling.

The tape recorder startled them. When I first turned it on, playing back their own voices, they leaped away. They understood what was being said, but didn't recognize their own voices & shouted back, puzzled & frightened.

But in an astonishingly short time, these villagers, including children & even a few women, were making movies themselves, taking Polaroid shots of each other, and endlessly playing with tape recorders. No longer fearful of their own portraits, men, wore them openly on their foreheads.

When we returned to Sio, months later, I thought at first we had made a wrong turn in the river network. I didn't recognize the place. Several houses had been rebuilt in a new style. Men wore European clothing. They carried themselves differently. They acted differently. Some had disappeared down river toward a government settlement, "wandering between two worlds/One dead, the other powerless to be born."

In one brutal movement they had been torn out of a tribal existence & transformed into detached individuals, lonely, frustrated, no longer at home—anywhere.

I fear our visit precipitated this crisis. Not our presence, but the presence of new media. A more isolated people might have been affected far less, perhaps scarcely at all. But the people of Sio were vulnerable. For a decade they had been moving imperceptibly toward Western culture. Our demonstration of media tipped the scales. Hidden changes suddenly coalesced & surfaced.

The effect was instant alienation. Their wits & sensibilities, released from tribal restraints, created a new identity: the private individual. For the first time, each man saw himself & his environment clearly and he saw them as separable.

Erich Kahler, in *The Tower and the Abyss*, speaks of the end result on German soldiers in World War II of a century of such conditioning to alienation; even during combat, they exhibited no sign of emotion, not even fear or hate: "these faces which had petrified into death masks."

It will immediately be asked if anyone has the right to do this to another human being, no matter what the reason. If this question is painful to answer when the situation is seen in microcosm, how is it answered when seen in terms of radio transmitters reaching hundreds of thousands of people daily, the whole process unexamined, undertaken blindly?

TECHNOLOGY IS EXPLICITNESS

When technology makes behavior explicit, the resulting images often seem more important—even sacred or obscene. Most people swear, but when they hear blasphemy or obscenity on film or radio, action becomes artifact, and the explicit artifact offends them more than the action itself.

We know little about this, other than the fact that it's true. Any technology, including language, can make reality frighteningly explicit, especially human reality. T. S. Eliot tells us that human beings cannot stand too much reality, by which he means, I assume, too much explicitness about reality. "A fearful thing is knowledge," says Tiresias in *Oedipus Rex*, "when to know helpeth no end."

It's a serious mistake to underestimate the trauma any new technology produces, especially any new communications technology. When people first encounter writing, they seem always to suffer great psychic dislocation. With speech, they hear consciousness, but with writing they see it. They suddenly experience a new way of being in relation to reality. "How do I know what to think," asks Alice, "till I see what I say?"

Seeing one's name for the first time can be electrifying. Isak Dinesen tells of recording a deposition for an illiterate Kikuyu:

132

When Jogona had at last come to the end of his tale, and I had got it all down, I told him that I was now going to read it to him. He turned away from me while I was reading, as if to avoid all distractions.

But as I read out his name . . . he swiftly turned his face to me, and gave me a great fierce flaming glance, so exuberant with laughter that it changed the old man into a boy, into the very symbol of youth. Again as I had finished the document and was reading out his name . . . the vital glance was repeated, this time deepened and calmed, with a new dignity.

Such a glance did Adam give the Lord when He formed him out of the dust, and breathed into his nostrils the breath of life, and man became a living soul. I had created him and shown him himself: Jogona Kanyagga of life everlasting. When I handed him the paper, he took it reverently and greedily, folded it up in a corner of his cloak and kept his hand upon it, and there was the proof of his existence. Here was something which Jogona Kanyagga had performed, and which would preserve his name for ever: the flesh was made word and dwelt among us full of grace and truth.

LOVE THY LABEL AS THYSELF

JOYCE

In the Middle Sepik, radios are common, tape recorders exist, and, though I saw no cameras, I met would-be camera owners.

Movies are occasionally shown by the government in certain villages. Without exception, the most popular films are those on New Guinea life. Villagers are aware that cameras can record their daily activities.

In Kandangan village the people became co-producers with us in making a film. The initial proposal came from us, but the actual filming of an initiation ceremony became largely their production.

In this area of the Sepik, the male initiation rite is absolutely forbidden to women, in the past on penalty of death. Our chief cameraman was a woman. It never occurred to us to ask if she might film: we assumed such a request would not only be denied, it would offend. But the Kandangan elders asked if she was good, and when told, "Yes, better than any of us," they requested that she operate one camera. Not only did they permit her inside the sacred enclosure, but they showed her where to position her equipment, helped her move it & delayed the ceremony while she reloaded. I'm convinced she was allowed to witness this rite, not because she was an outsider, but solely because her presence was necessary for the production of the best possible film.

The initiates were barely conscious at the end of their ordeal, but they grinned happily when shown Polaroid shots of their scarified backs. The elders asked to have the sound track played back to them. They then asked that the film be brought back & projected, promising to erect another sacred enclosure for the screening.

Finally they announced that this was the last involuntary initiation & they offered for sale their ancient water drums, the most sacred objects of this ceremony. Film threatened to replace a ceremony hundreds, perhaps thousands, of years old.

Yet film could never fulfill the ceremony's original function. That function was to test young men for manhood & weld them forever into a closed, sacred society. Now the ceremony, and by an extension the entire society, could be put on a screen before them, detached from them. They could watch themselves. No one who ever comes to know himself with the detachment of an observer is ever the same again.

Postcript: When the film was not finished within the promised time & hence not shown in the village, involuntary initiations were resumed.

TO SEE OURSELVES AS OTHERS SEE US

To offset a serious protein deficiency, powdered milk was introduced into the diet of New Guinea schoolchildren. But the children didn't like the milk. So a live cow was taken on tour, milked in front of them & the milk distributed in glasses. But again they grimaced & laughed & rejected it.

Miss Juanita Ferguson, a teacher in the Southern Highlands, filmed these reactions. Her students loved the films. They asked to see them over & over. Each student especially wanted to see himself—to see the funny face he had made & watch the reactions of others to his humor.

At which point, much of the resistance to milk disappeared.

Children everywhere are fascinated by pictures of themselves, far more so than by pictures of friends. They know what friends look like, but they've never seen themselves. They're also more interested in their own art work than in the art work of others. The work of another is simply part of the environment, but their own work is visible proof of what was hitherto, for them, merely an inner thought, a psychic experience. Now part of them is visible to themselves & for a moment, at least, it gives them new identity. Then gradually it becomes subject to environmental control. Any environment has the power to distort or deflect human awareness. Photographs increase self-awareness only as long as they are private & not part of the environment.

OF COURSE IN THIS YOU FELLOWS
SEE MORE THAN I COULD SEE. YOU SEE ME.

Joseph Conrad, *Heart of Darkness*

Responses to the camera & recorder ranged from total incomprehension among the Biami, to keen sophistication among young political leaders in the cities.

The Biami at first had no idea what cameras were. That is, they had no idea cameras made pictures. They thought cameras simply stored pictures. To them, Polaroid cameras were boxes containing images of themselves, while movie cameras were boxes with windows into which we peered. We encouraged them to sight through viewfinders, assuming they might at least gain the notion of a telescope. But I don't think they understood even this & they continually wrecked one scene after another by walking in front of cameras, standing in front of them, above all peering into them. Time & again, right in the middle of a superb sequence, I would suddenly see an eyeball coming directly into the camera.

In the Highlands, however, and even in the Middle Sepik, most villagers know what cameras are & the moment they see one pointed at them, their behavior changes. This change is far more pronounced than that produced by awareness that one is simply being observed. A camera holds the potential for *self*-viewing, *self*-awareness.

Using long lenses, we filmed people who were unaware

of our presence. Then one of us stepped from concealment & stood watching, but not interrupting their activity. Finally the cameraman set up his equipment in full view, urging everyone to go on with whatever he was doing. Almost invariably, body movements became faster, jerky, without poise or confidence. Faces that had been relaxed froze or alternated between twitching & rigidity.

Thus we had sequences showing people who, in their own minds, were: (1) unobserved, (2) being observed by a stranger, (3) being recorded on film which they later might see. There was little difference between (1) & (2), but (3) was quite different.

Before we learned better, we asked people to repeat actions just observed but missed in filming. It was hopeless. Subjects were willing enough, but their self-conscious performances bore little resemblance to their unconscious behavior. Among the hundreds of subjects filmed in a variety of situations, I cannot recall a single person familiar with a camera who was capable of ignoring it. This makes me wonder about ethnographic films generally. Even where subjects are accomplished actors, how does their acting compare with their behavior when no cameras are present? We may compliment their acting, but is it the theatrical performance we admire or their true-to-life impersonation?

When Joshua Whitcomb, a 19th century actor, performed in Keene, New Hampshire, the audience demanded its money back. It couldn't understand being charged admission. On stage, Whitcomb was exactly the same as any number of local citizens who could be seen daily without charge. Said a representative in protest: "It warn't no acting; it was just a lot of fellers goin' around and doin' things."

Since most ethnographic films profess to record just that—people going around doing things—the question arises: do they? Or has the camera produced changes in behavior we can't see because they are so common among us, so much a part of our lives that we fail to recognize them as alien in others? Do we take self-awareness for granted?

138

For New Guinea, the record is clear: comparing footage of a subject who is unaware of a camera, then aware of it—fully aware of it as an instrument for self-viewing, self-examination—is comparing different behavior, different persons.

MOMENTS PRESERVED

Irving Penn took a series of extraordinary photographs at the 1970 Goroka Agricultural Show, a great gathering of tribes held annually in the Highlands, attended by thousands of villagers, many elaborately plumed & painted.

As usual, Penn employed a collapsible, portable studio with one wall open & the camera outside, looking in. The secret of this studio is that it created its own space—space without background.

The moment subjects stepped across that threshold, they changed totally. All confusion & excitement ceased. Even those outside became still. A sudden intensity possessed everyone.

The same subjects who moments before posed comically for tourists, affecting exaggerated poses, now behaved with intense concentration. Their bodies became rigid, their muscles tense; their fingers tightly gripped whatever they touched. When Penn repositioned them, he found their bodies stiff in a way he never found subjects in our society.

The crowd outside, looking in, also became rigid. Chaos ceased & the scene became a tableau.

If this were merely my account, it might easily be dismissed as something contrived to fit the thesis of this book. But I have tried to record here, as best I remember them, Penn's own words. And the evidence is also in the photographs.

These photographs aren't anthropological documents in the usual sense. They don't record moments out of daily life. No captions explaining decorations or describing ceremonies would be relevant. Absolutely nothing that can be said about the culture or personality of the subjects is pertinent to their pictures. What holds us, fascinates us, is their stance and, above all, their eyes.

A camera is the ideal instrument for preserving the momentary art of body decoration & face paint. But ordinary photographs can preserve such art. These photographs are not ordinary. Penn has captured something so elusive, so momentary, that were it not for the fact the camera created it, it's unlikely a camera could record it.

And even now, with that elusive something captured & spread before us, we scarcely know what to make of it. One thing is certain: on every face, even the faces of children, there is fear. Not fear of camera or cameraman. Not ordinary fear.

If this were ordinary fear, subjects would be glancing for reassurance toward companions outside. Instead, they stare at the lens.

Nor is this the fear of those who, seeing their images for the first time, cover their mouths to preserve their identities. For participants at the Goroka Fair, that was past history. Most knew a good deal about cameras. They knew their spirits were so powerful they could do more than cast a reflection on a mirror; they could leave a permanent imprint on that mirror, an imprint that would preserve forever this moment, this man.

The terror in their eyes is the tribal terror of being recognized as individuals.

Bedecked in barbaric splendor once designed to strike fear into enemies & humility into rivals, these ex-warriors asked to be recorded for posterity. Yet what we see is not fearful expressions, but expressions of fear combined with an exaltation that confers an awesome dignity on every subject. We see men at the very moment they voluntarily leave everything familiar & step forever into limbo, going through that vanishing point alone & going through it wideawake.

When Alice went through that looking glass, Victorians called her a fairy-tale figure, but the coming of new media meant we would all go through that vanishing point from which none return unchanged.

Now it was the New Guineans' turn.

Everyone who watched understood. Those outside kept their eyes on the subjects, while subjects kept their eyes on the lens. They never looked at Penn, nor to one side, nor at those outside. Their eyes fixed unwaveringly on that single point, no matter how long the session. That point was the point men enter when they leave this world behind & step alone, absolutely alone, into limbo. That was the source of their terror & exaltation & intense self-awareness.

One sees that some intensity in Matthew Brady's Civil War photographs; in portraits of Indians in the Old West; in Renaissance paintings of unsmiling dukes staring down eternity. Our eyebeams lock with those of strangers at some timeless, spaceless point. Those eyes stare back at us with an intensity we seldom encounter today in the portraits of our smiling leaders & graduating seniors.

Rembrandt was said to be the first great master whose sitters sometimes dreaded seeing their portraits. Perhaps one reason we could never produce another Rembrandt is that we no longer produce such sitters.

The technology that lifted man out of both his environment & his body, allowing him to enter & leave limbo at will, has now become so casual, so environmental, we make that trip with the numbness of commuters, our eyes unseeing, the mystery of self-confrontation & self-discovery gone.

PORTRAITS

I think precisely the type of studio Irving Penn employed, where subjects are photographed in limbo, using a good camera & sealing prints in clear plastic, should be set up all through New Guinea. Its primary virtue would be as counterforce to radio.

It is one of the ironies of change in New Guinea that the introduction of the camera, though traumatic & disruptive of tribal life, must now be encouraged to offset the even greater trauma & disruption caused by radio. Human sensory balance must now be sought in terms of media balance.

A photograph moves us toward the isolated moment. It arrests time. It exists in pure space. It emphasizes individuality, private identity, and confers an element of permanence on that image. In many ways, it's the exact opposite of radio.

Such studios could easily become self-supporting, providing indigenous employment. Interest is already there.

We used up a great quantity of film during a six-week stay in Mintima, a Chimbu village in the Central Highlands. It became widely known we would take anyone's photograph, free, and there was always a crowd waiting. Many walked considerable distances. I recall a policeman who walked fifteen miles only to encounter rain, so he returned the next day, walking a total of sixty miles for one picture.

A photographic portrait, when new & privately possessed, promotes identity, individualism: it offers opportunities for self-recognition, self-study. It provides the extra sensation of objectivizing the self. It makes that self more real, more dramatic. For the subject, it's no longer enough to be: now he *knows* he *is*. He is conscious of himself.

Until man becomes conscious of his personal appearance & his private identity, there is little self-expression.

Sartre, in *The Words*, speaks of his mother: "Anne Marie, the younger daughter, spent her childhood on a chair. She was taught to be bored, to sit up straight, to sew. She was gifted: the family thought it distinguished to leave her gifts underdeveloped; she was radiant: they hid the fact from her . . . beauty was beyond their means . . . fifty years later, when turning the pages of a family album, Anne Marie realized that she had been beautiful."

In New Guinea, subjects who understood what a camera was & chose to pose before it generally faced the camera directly. But a few of the elders offered their profiles. I recall one elderly man, dressed as a warrior, who turned to one side & began to shout toward the horizon. I had the feeling this posture derived from some ancient battlefield.

One day at a marriage ceremony, we offered to photograph the bridal couple. The groom immediately posed with a male friend. We re-posed him with his pregnant bride & year-old child. Some weeks later we visited their home & saw this photograph carefully pinned up.

Actually, the incident was infinitely more complicated than this brief account indicates. It was instantly obvious from the behavior of everyone present that the picture he had requested would have been routine, whereas the picture we took was anything but routine. It was as if we had photographed, in our society, the groom kissing the best man. All the power & prestige of the camera had been used in direct conflict with one of the deepest cultural values of this Highland New Guinea society.

If I were a missionary, dedicated to promoting & preserving

144

the Christian family, I would buy the biggest camera I could find, photograph all wedding couples & supply each with a large print, elaborately framed.

In our own culture, the sanctity & reality of marriage was declared as much in wedding photographs as it was in written documents. I think the power of such pictures would be even greater in New Guinea.

Since I'm not a missionary, not dedicated to promoting alien values at the expense of indigenous ones, I offer this as an illustration & speculation, not as a recommendation.

PHOTOGRAPHIC COMIC BOOKS

Photography emphasizes the world of pure sight: continuity, gradations, shadings. No intervals, no interface. The latter belong to touch, not sight, and are expressed visually by cartoon & hard-edge art, not photography.

Cartoon art, in comic books, posters & ads, has been introduced into village life, borrowed indiscriminately from Western culture—the only consideration having been content. The tactile effects of such art, however appropriate to the sensory life of contemporary Western man, are hardly needed in New Guinea life where tactile experience needs no reinforcement. What is needed to offset radio is visual models. To this end, I would replace cartoons with photographs, especially in posters & where possible in ads. I would also create comic books where each scene is a photograph with "conversation balloons" pasted on top. Such comic books are easily designed, inexpensively printed, & capable of producing effects quite different from those produced by either cartoons or radio, though the content of all three might be identical.

Two-dimensional perspective permits many times, many spaces, but three-dimensional perspective permits only one time, one space. The realistic expression of a photographic portrait records a single moment in time, observed from a single point in space.

CLOSING ONE EYE

When we taught the Biami how to use cameras, they found it difficult, at times impossible, to close one eye at a time. There was much fumbling as they held down one eyelid with one hand while trying to hold & operate a camera with the other. Sometimes friends assisted by holding down an eyelid, allowing them the use of both hands.

Closing one eye soon became a daily game. One morning a group approached us, pushing one man ahead. He stepped forward, grinned broadly and—to the delight of his companions—closed one eye. Soon the big wink became a daily greeting.

Very young children have difficulty closing one eye. I believe this is characteristic of most, perhaps all, illiterates. The ability to close one eye at a time seems to be associated with literacy. Literacy involves a unique sensory pattern. It shatters the "natural" orchestration of the senses & permits far greater control over individual senses, especially when one sense is used in isolation.

I've never been impressed by the marksmanship of natives—until they learn to read. The T. E. Lawrence myth of the romantic Englishman leading an illiterate army of deadly sharpshooters is just that: romantic myth. A rifle in the hands of an illiterate can be a deadly weapon, but for the wrong reasons. Illiterates rarely use the safety as

147

if it were an eyelid, that is, lift it only when the rifle is visually on target. As a result, accidental discharges are common & premature firing is standard.

Native hunters rely upon their considerable skills as trackers. They often know how to get in close to animals before shooting. Here the bow can be preferable to the rifle, for it's quiet & if a hunter misses, he may get another chance.

Most Canadian Indians, in my experience, prefer not to hunt with dogs, for if a hunter misses his first shot or merely wounds the animal, dogs pursue it. Otherwise the wounded animal flees only a short distance, then lies down to lick its wound. A sensible hunter pauses to brew tea, knowing the animal's muscles will tighten up & that he is likely to get another shot.

Under certain circumstances, good marksmanship can be a disadvantage. During certain seasons, seals lose their fat & buoyancy: if a hunter kills one from too great a distance, it sinks before he reaches it.

A rifle is an extension of the eye: the marksman conceives of himself as a point in space, separated by a middle distance from his target, another point in space. He connects the two by sight, making adjustments for wind, if necessary, but ideally limiting the experience to a highly specialized use of the eye: focused sight. He tracks his moving target the way a reader scans a printed line.

Great marksmanship is probably a by-product of literacy. Literate American colonists, who outshot illiterate British regulars, lengthened the British musket, rifled its barrel, and added front & rear sights to create the Kentucky rifle.

The compass, used for navigation, and artillery, used with precision, belong to literate man: both are extensions of the reader's eye.

THE PHYSIOLOGY OF LITERACY

The capacity to separate the senses & use the eye alone for reading is not instantly conferred on readers. Parallels with what is now occurring in New Guinea can be found in Western man's past. Thus in the Middle Ages, reading was aloud, often as song, and frequently in unison with readers standing & gesturing. Silent, lonely reading was a long time in coming. In *Confessions*, St. Augustine wrote:

> When Ambrose read, his eyes moved over the pages, and his soul penetrated the meaning, without his uttering a word or moving his tongue. Many times—for no one was forbidden to enter, or announced to him—we saw him reading silently and never otherwise, and after a while we would go away, conjecturing that during the brief interval he used to refresh his spirit, free from the tumult of the business of others, he did not wish to be disturbed, for perhaps he feared that some-one who was listening, hearing a difficult part of the text, might ask him to explain an obscure passage or might wish to discuss it with him, and would thus prevent him from reading as many volumes as he desired. I believe that he read that way to preserve his voice, which was easily strained. In any case, whatever the man's purpose was, it was surely a good one.

As Borges points out, St. Augustine was a disciple of

St. Ambrose, Bishop of Milan around the year 384. Thirteen years later in Munidia, when he wrote his *Confessions*, that singular spectacle still troubled him: a man in a room, with a book, reading without articulating the words.

Even today, reading isn't wholly a visual experience. Physicians forbid patients who have undergone throat surgery to read. In Yugoslavia, an unsuccessful attempt was recently made to "mind-read" by attaching wires to vocal cords.

When Russian children in an experiment were told to keep their mouths open, they made six times as many spelling mistakes as they made normally: they couldn't "say" the words to themselves. Chinese children, whose words are pictorial rather than phonetic, aren't affected in this way. Chinese injured in the acoustic area of the brain don't lose their ability to write.

Where the letters of an alphabet closely match the phonemes or minimal sound units of a language, it's easy to teach reading, and spelling is never a problem, but speed reading is difficult: readers are slowed down by inwardly experiencing the sounds of words. Thus the lack of close correspondence between the phonemes of English & the Latin alphabet favors speed reading (though it delays reading-learning & makes spelling a problem), whereas in Spanish & Italian, where graphemes & phonemes more closely correspond, speed reading is more difficult.

Small children with reading problems are sometimes encouraged to sing-dance words as they learn to spell them. Music is widely used as background for teaching penmanship. Similarly, it was found in South Africa that the Kalahari learned more quickly to ride bicycles when a musical accompaniment was provided.

In shifting from speech to writing, man gave up an ear for an eye, and transferred his interest from spiritual to spatial, from reverential to referential. God became "The One on High," and all inner psychological states were described as outer perceptions. We said "thereafter," not the logical *thenafter;* "always," meaning *all ways,* for *all times;* "before,"

151

meaning *in front of,* for *earlier.* Language & perception shifted to the spatial, the observable, the *seen.* Chaytor, in *From Script to Print,* writes:

When we speak or write, ideas evoke acoustic images, combined with kinesthetic images, which are at once transferred into visual images. The speaker or writer can now hardly conceive of language except in printed and written form; the reflex actions by which the process of reading and writing is performed have become so "instinctive" and are performed with such facile rapidity, that the change from the auditory to the visual is concealed from the reader or writer, and makes analysis of it a matter of great difficulty. It may be that the acoustic and kinesthetic images are inseparable, and that "image" as such is an abstraction made for purposes of analysis, but which is non-existent considered in itself and as pure.

REVERSING SOUND

"We should remember," writes Freud, "how fond children are of playing at reversing the sound of words, and how frequently the dream-work makes use of various ends of a reversal of the material. . . ."

In Sio we taught a number of people to use tape recorders. They quickly learned to distort sound: magnify it, speed it up & slow it down, and especially to reverse it. They delighted in discovering both hidden resources in language & new dimensions in sound.

Several children imitated the reversed speech they heard when tapes were rewound. On their own initiative they recorded these imitations, then played them backward, successfully achieving intelligibility.

I've heard children in our own society do precisely this same thing with great success. The explanation lies, I think, in the sensory profiles of oral peoples, many of whom possess uncanny skill in miming sound patterns. One notices this in the ease with which they learn songs, including songs in alien languages.

Charlie Chaplin was able to mime reversed speech he heard on sound tracks. When these imitations were recorded & played back in reverse, whole phrases were intelligible. He also acted out film scenes in reverse. When the film was run backward, the scene became comprehensible, though his movements were strangely unnatural.

In the 17th century English witchcraft trials, it was commonly asserted that the Devil appeared in the form of a Dog—that is, God backward. The English still employ this same metathesis when they refer to a clergyman's collar as a "dog collar" instead of a "God collar."

The Black Mass of the Middle Ages was often no more than the Mass recited backward. Divorce was achieved by performing the marriage ceremony backward.

Boustrophedon, the ancient mode of writing alternate lines in opposite directions, added to the possibilities for reversed language.

WORDS IN SPACE

When people first encounter writing, they often play with words, as if words were newly discovered things, subject to limitless spatial rearrangement. The multilevel complexity of oral language is not immediately lost with the coming of literacy: instead, it is shifted to spatial configurations.

Written words do, of course, exist in space & can be physically rearranged. This discovery often leads to the invention of spatial word games. These have been popular in many cultures, especially where literacy is fresh & numerology, astrology & alchemy are professional pursuits.

Vestiges of such games survive in our culture. We have the palidromes ABLE WAS I ERE I SAW ELBA, Napoleon's lament, and MADAM, I'M ADAM, allegedly man's first statement. Both read the same backward & forward. James Thurber's NOW NO SWIMS ON MON reads the same upside down.

Words may be read downward, as in street signs, or in the vertical columns of crossword puzzles, or in acrostic verse where the initial letters of each line of a poem, taken together, form a word or name.

Words may be concealed within words: "Her very C's, her U's, 'n' her T's" (*Twelfth Night*, *II:88*).

In a rear mirror, ECNALUBMA reads AMBULANCE,

while through the windshield $\frac{ING}{X}$ reads CROSSING.

A letter sent to Wood
John
Mass
was allegedly delivered to John Underwood, Andover, Massachusetts.

We sometimes convert telephone & postal numbers into words, for words are easier to remember, e.g., the telephone number NERVOUS, the New York City number giving the correct time.

The letters of the early Hebrew alphabet also served as numerals: scribes played at making combined word-mathematical statements.

In New Guinea, I was particularly interested in graffiti, doodles, signs combining words, in symbols & pictures, bulletin-board notices, private letters, scribblings chalked on school blackboards after hours, etc. There was abundant material to fill my interest. Even students who had mastered penmanship sometimes departed from sequential order to fill space by wholly different means. The spatial logic of local signs often had to be discovered, but once discovered, was usually clear & sometimes ingenious.

I think this aspect of language should be given maximum encouragement in New Guinea, not only as a means of furthering literacy, but as a means of muting radio. I see radio as potentially very dangerous, especially where it lacks serious competition from other media. Radio's role in North Africa & Indonesia should serve as a warning. In each place, it broke down small, traditional tribes, then retribalized the populations as a whole, building nationalism to a feverish pitch & creating unreasonable national goals & consumer hopes. Radio simply does not promote the sort of social structure & economic specialization necessary for an increase both in living standard & military might, though both are easily promised via airwaves.

Those who control the content of radio take such arguments

lightly. To them, what matters is what radio *says*. To me, what matters is what radio *does*. They regard radio as a neutral instrument & place full responsibility for its use on people. I see nothing "neutral" about my technology. To me, all technologies are human extensions & those extensions create different people.

Radio in New Guinea could easily come to dominate the sensory lives of the village people. If the government insists on its expansion, then I think support should be given to activities that favor individualism, specialization, privacy, enclosed space, etc., that is, activities producing effects opposite from those produced by radio. Print, of course, comes first to mind. But accelerating the current literacy program would require major financing, as well as create its own problems. I think a great deal could be achieved, with minimum expenditure, by promoting abstract spatial games.

For example, I would promote chess. Chess is an art of pure location. A player must sequentially reorder units & unit clusters by visualizing how they would look in a succession of subsequent spaces. The chessman lie "out there," but future moves must lie in graphic clarity in the player's mind.

The rules of chess are easily learned, yet as George Steiner notes, "There are more possible variants in a game at chess than it is calculated there are atoms in this sprawling universe. The number of possible legitimate ways of playing the first four moves on each side comes to 318,979,584,000. Playing one game a minute and never repeating it, the entire population of the globe would need two hundred and sixteen billion years to exhaust all conceivable ways of playing the first ten moves."

Chess might find a waiting audience in New Guinea. Interest is often high in cultures where literacy is fresh & no single medium is dominant. Chess requires negligible equipment. Any space serves. Players need nothing in common, save love of chess, for chess is unrelated to culture, language,

157

age. Along with music & mathematics, it is one of the few fields in which there are child prodigies. It doesn't derive from the world "out there" & cannot be translated into that world. It doesn't prepare people for employment and this, too, at the moment is an advantage, for in New Guinea it's easier to prepare people for employment than to provide employment.

Unlike cards, chess is rarely played for money. It's a game of pure skill, not chance, and therefore without appeal to gamblers.

Obviously, chess by itself is hardly a sufficient counterforce to radio. But combined with a number of other media, each of which favors visual space or segmented time, I think it should be promoted. By "other media" I specifically mean: literacy; portrait photography; photo comic books; crossword puzzles; huge mirrors erected in public places; aerial photographs of villages, displayed in those villages beneath clocks that signal the hour; etc.

Such suggestions are certain to amuse administrators who place their faith in technology & good intentions. But in a small way they could help correct sensory & psychic imbalances created by radio. Obviously nothing is going to turn off radio, but its effects can be turned down within the interior environment of the self.

YOU CAN'T SAY "NO" PICTORIALLY

It's easy to say "No" verbally. Words are neutral symbols which stand for a reality but do not resemble that reality.

A picture, however, often resembles reality, especially when that picture moves. This makes pictorial media enormously persuasive. It requires an act of will to disbelieve what one sees & an even greater will to accept the reverse of what one sees.

The New Guinea government circulated large posters that said: Protect Our Rare Birdwing Butterflies; and beneath this, pictures of the butterflies in question, along with the warning: "$200 fine for collecting; $20 penalty per specimen in possession thereof." Villagers immediately collected these butterflies & took them to agricultural officers for payment.

A common beer ad in New Guinea shows a foaming glass with the caption: Be Specific, Say South Pacific. When the sale of beer was permitted to indigenes, the London Missionary Society posted identical ads, except for the caption: Say No. Beer sales immediately increased. Drinkers ordered No.

The government produced a film called *Stori Bilong Stilman*, which showed a village youth committing five thefts. In the last, while an accomplice distracts a shopkeeper, the thief fills a bag & then the two go outside where they happily

159

eat the pilfered food & divide the stolen money. Audiences were delighted. The thief, of course, was arrested & taken to jail, but the message was clear: stealing is fun, easy, rewarding & this is the way it's done.

I suspect crime increased wherever the film was shown. I do know that the lead actor was soon in prison, convicted of precisely the crime he played in the last scene.

There seemed to be one example, however, that contradicted this theory that one can't say "No" pictorially. It was a most effective sign, seen everywhere throughout the Territory, depicting a human hand, & meaning *Imtambut*, taboo, private. At first I thought it meant Do Not Touch & depicted a hand laid on, the idea being Don't Do This. But a hand is a visual pun: in outline or silhouette, palm & back are identical. These warning signs didn't show hands touching forbidden objects; they threatened trespassers. Villagers perceived them as palms thrust into the faces of intruders, like the hand of a traffic policeman.

Could this explain hands painted by Paleolithic artists on the walls of cave sanctuaries? The hand motif was also prevalent in North American Indian art, especially on masks & shields.

TECHNOLOGY AS ENVIRONMENT

Technology is explicitness—when technology is new. That same technology, which once defined identity, even created individualism, can in time erode & dissolve identity until it merges once more with its environment.

President Kennedy's signature was done for him by a machine which so exactly reproduced the hand signing his name that experts cannot distinguish between his real signature & the mechanical ones. Malcolm Muggeridge tells how, in the excitement & distress of the Dallas tragedy, no one remembered to turn the machine off. So, the president went on signing "personalized" letters after he was dead.

Technology plucks a man from the engulfing web of society & environment, allows him to see himself in isolation, to examine himself in depth. Then slowly, inexorably, it swallows him, binding him to technology as tightly as society ever held him. Where once he knew himself through others, now he knows himself through images over which he generally exerts little control.

"One only knows that one exists," wrote Goethe, "if one rediscovers oneself in others."

Our fascination with the life & death of Marilyn Monroe derives, I think, from the fact that media stole her soul, took away all personal identity until the only private act left to her was suicide.

Knowledge of media alone is not sufficient protection from them. The moment Marshall McLuhan shifted from private media analyst to public media participant, he was converted into an image the media manipulated & exploited.

As long as the Yippies used media for their own ends, they were wild power loose in the land. When Abbie Hoffman announced the invention of a counterweapon to Mace, the network cameras assembled and two Yippies, male & female, sprayed each other from purple cans labeled Love, tore off their clothes & engaged in intercourse. Newsmen protested, "We can't use that." At this point, Hoffman was in command. But when David Frost said, "Abbie, we have to pause for a commercial," the Yippie revolution was over & Hoffman left for the Virgin Islands.

New media allow us to escape from old environments, but soon imprison us in new environments, namely themselves. For one brief moment we have a clear image of ourselves & our environment, both hitherto invisible because they were too close. They became visible by becoming obsolete.

The appearance of the telegraph & onset of the electronic age allowed Marx to see the structure of the past economic system & Freud to see the nature of literate individualism. Both viewed man & society as separable, in opposition. These were backward glances, the views of men dissatisfied with what they saw in the past, but with no awareness that new environments soon would surround them.

IMAGE MANIPULATION

Throughout New Guinea, it's commonly feared that if one's name or image falls into the hands of an enemy, he may use it mischievously. Sorcerers believe they can render even the mightiest helpless by naming, or injure another by introducing his likeness into an unpleasant situation. A sorcerer who possesses any part of his victim, anything once *him*—hair clippings, footprints, etc.—has him at his mercy.

The concept of soul-stealing applies in modern life, as well. John Grierson, the Scottish filmmaker, once warned, "You may take a man's soul away by taking a picture of him. You may take part of his privacy away."

There is a widespread saying among American Indians, "Traders stole our furs, settlers our lands, now missionaries want our souls." I recently heard an Indian say this on TV. He was on guard against the missionaries; in the meantime he let the media capture & possess his spirit totally.

Once a spirit or image falls into the hands of another, he's free to do with it as he likes.

In 1950, a Baltimore tabloid ran a photomontage of Earl Browder, the communist leader, and Millard Tydings, the Maryland senator, though the two had never met or been associated. Putting Tyding's image in this context helped destroy him politically.

THE MAGIC OF RADIO

In New Guinea, those who control the content of radio seek to replace magic with rationalism. They don't declare this openly, of course: rationalists never welcome the missionary label. Nevertheless, it's their goal. They treat radio as an extension of book culture & proceed as if its format were unrelated to its effects. But the *content* & *goals* of the programs they produce are far removed from the *effects* of these programs.

One of radio's main effects is the promotion of pure spirit. No dream experience, no ancient religion ever separated spirit from flesh more effectively than the electronic media. Speech & writing also divorce image from object, but electronic media magnify this process astronomically.

Separation of spirit from flesh, hitherto limited in New Guinea to dream-myth-ritual, now occurs daily, promoted by the government. Striving to introduce rational thought into village life via radio, administrators have chosen a medium singularly unsuited to this particular message.

If I understand rationalism correctly, its basic elements —lineality, temporality, causality, individualism—are, if not actual by-products of literacy, certainly more at home in this medium than in any other. The question, Should rationalism be promoted in New Guinea? is not within the

165

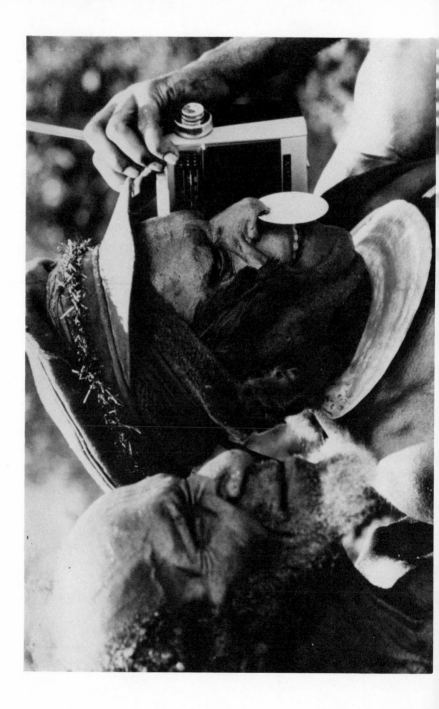

scope of my inquiry. But the question, How effective are electronic media in promoting rationalism? is. In New Guinea, those who think they are promoting rationalism are actually promoting something quite different, something they secretly admire more—electronic technology. Their intention is simply to use electronic media to extend the benefits of rationalism. But the effect is what counts, not the intent. By concentrating on content & ignoring effect, administrators remain oblivious to one of radio's principal achievements: it promotes magical systems where images, separated from bodies, exist purely in time, without spatial identity.

Electronic media everywhere produce this effect. In the United States, the young partly offset this effect by emphasizing sensate experience: spiced foods, sex, nudity, wine, hair, bare feet, tactility, body arts, private conversations, etc.

Of course, none of these primary experiences needs to be reawakened in New Guinea. But with the intrusion of electronic images into village life, sensate experience is devalued.

Elvis Presley's voice & face are popular in many parts of New Guinea, but neither he nor any of the other stars whose songs many of the young know by heart have ever set foot on this island. They are truly stars: pure spirits whose very purity makes them environmental & therefore immediately acceptable.

CULTURAL UNEMPLOYMENT

The *New York Times* (August 15, 1971) reports that Indonesia's musicians are slowly finding themselves out of work. The traditional gamelan music can still be heard at night all over central Java, but the chances are good that the music comes from tape recorders. Orchestras have decreased in number & instruments gather dust.

For about $13, an orchestra of 12 can be hired for a performance that may last eight hours. Included is the cost of transporting more than a ton of bulky instruments by horse or oxcart.

For less than $8, young men on motorcycles or in a borrowed truck speed down with loudspeakers, tape recorder & tapes of the best gamelan orchestras in Indonesia. They can be ready for action in minutes. Most of the music they offer is traditional, but not all: the recorded music of John Lennon was played at an all-night celebration for the birth of a child.

To many villagers, especially the young, the new, fancy electronic equipment is more exciting than a group of old men with ancient instruments. Not many youths are learning to play & carry on the art form.

Aside from the merits of a live performance & a performer's art, other questions arise. What are the old men going to do with their time? What other activities will give them equal satisfaction?

In New Guinea, such questions are serious, for already economic unemployment is a major problem & to this is now being added cultural unemployment.

AND I CAME INTO THE FIELDS AND WIDE PALACES OF MEMORY.

St. Augustine

Both the Australian Broadcasting Corporation (ABC) & the administration network run by the Department of Information and Extension Services (DIES) produce first-rate programs for the education & entertainment of the local population. But that population is so incredibly diverse that strange messages often reach strange ears.

Radio in New Guinea opens with a Moral Rearmament chorus and for the rest of the day the airwaves are a *Finnegans Wake:* native sacred songs made public; Voice of America on Tricia Nixon's fashions; country music; Peking Radio on anti-Stalin revisionists; Christian fundamentalism; local news; stock exchange reports; an interview with a 76-year-old choreographer on the status of Australian ballet; frequent racing reports, etc., etc.

Radio's chance juxtapositions lead to interesting interpretations: I heard a Fundamentalist's sermon on Lucifer, Prince of Light, fallen from Grace but still titular head of the City on Earth, followed by a news broadcast on smog, riots, power failures, crime, hunger—the City as Purgatory.

At Barapidgin, a remote village on the Wagameri, I picked up a broadcast direct from Apollo 11. The interpreter, a Christian convert, listened intently & then said, "Getting

170

closer to God is good." Apparently Wernher von Braun shared his assumption that man was voyaging to other planets to search for God, for in this same broadcast he said, "Through a closer look at the Creation, we ought to gain a better understanding of the Creator."

In the Mt. Hagen theater, cowboy & horror films are immensely popular. No audience of New Jersey wrestling fans can equal this Highland audience for sheer frenzy: screaming, on their feet, most standing on seats.

In one remote area I saw a tattooed, skewered-nosed, feathered, painted, armed audience, including one local beauty nursing a piglet, watch their first movie: one film was an interview with the British Foreign Secretary on the 1957 German Arms Treaty. Another dealt with the use of closed-circuit TV for traffic control in Sidney. I have no idea what these villagers thought of a film on elderly Australian ladies flying kites.

But in a deeper sense, it didn't matter. What mattered was that these media were changing the environment itself.

THE WORLD IS TOO MUCH WITH US

The senior administrators in DIES, the agency sponsoring my work, were decent types, but rather limited. Their notion of communications was the sermon, preferably sermons on sanitation, respect for authority, etc. To them, radio & film were simply efficient ways to convey information to the uninformed. They spoke of themselves as practical men, by which they meant they believed in experience. Talk of invisible media effects was dismissed. In the meantime they filled the airwaves with information.

A closed society might be defined as a society enjoying a tight correlation between information & behavior: the information needed for proper behavior is at hand, and no other.

An open society would then be one where information is available for various forms of behavior: the individual selects his information & thereby determines his behavior.

What, then, do we call a society that provides incredible masses of information, little of which can be translated into behavior? The "spurious society"? A genuine culture, wrote Edward Sapir, is the "expression of a . . . consistent attitude toward life, an attitude which sees the significance of any one element of civilization in its relation to all others. It is, ideally speaking, a culture in which nothing is spiritually meaningless."

172

Radio in New Guinea is totally meaningless to many who hear it for the simple reason it reaches them in languages they don't understand. Even when it is understood, much of it is inapplicable to their lives. And even where information is applicable, how much, in fact, can be applied? Are there really that many job opportunities to justify releasing that much information into the environment?

Western man has developed very complex means of dealing with the great masses of information that move freely through his environment. Western scientists, for example, developed the technique of suspended judgment, by which no information is suppressed, but none acted on rashly. Most New Guineans have no such means.

IDEAS IN THE PLAYPEN

W. H. R. Rivers reports that in small groups in Polynesia & Melanesia, decisions are often arrived at & acted upon, though never formulated by anybody. The Western observer, listening to the proceedings of a native council, realizes after a while that the original topic in dispute has changed. Inquiring when they are going to decide the question in which he is interested, he is told "that it had already been decided and that they had passed on to other business. The decision had been made with none of the processes by which our councils or committees decide disputed points. The members of the council have become aware at a certain point that they are in agreement, and it was not necessary to bring the agreement explicitly to notice."

Separation of oratory from decision-making isn't unique to Melanesians. People long familiar with Westminster democracy accept that there is a large element of play in it.

Democracy, as we know it, developed under literacy. One essential element of literacy is separation of thought from emotion & behavior.

Speech everywhere combines phonemes (sound units), tonemes (tonal units), and kines (body units). Some linguists prefer to study phonemes alone, but tonemes (which favor the expression of emotions) and kines (which are actual body movements) remain integral parts of speech. They are especially important in nonliterate languages. Ultimately, it's impossible to separate word from thought, thought from emotion, emotion from behavior.

In oral societies, perception or cognition is associated with, or immediately followed by, an "emotion." Every idea is not only a state of knowing but a tendency toward movement: "To see her is to love her"; "I shuddered at the thought."

Emotion effects both heart & lungs. "Every emotion quickens the action of the heart and with it the respiration," observed Darwin. "When a fearful object is before us we pant and cannot deeply inhale."

Emotion tends to beget bodily motion. In Homer, the manliest warriors wept openly, beat their chests, tore their hair, and when this was sung about in the Athenian marketplace, it's probable that listeners joined in the expression of these emotions.

Hearing these accounts meant experiencing them. But one can *read* them without emotion. Any newspaper front page is a mass of tragedies, yet we read unmoved. We could never act or dance such tragedies without emotion. Nor sing them. Nor express them as poetry. But reading is different. Silent reading is thinking deserted by emotion. It leads to a high degree of separation of mental concepts from the plurality of the concrete.

Perhaps all people find it necessary to separate, to some extent, group decision-making from oratory & emotion. New Guinea administrators struggle with this problem when they seek to dilute the tone of political criticism. In principle, they offer opposition parties the right to be heard on radio; in practice, they often present that criticism as faulty, something best corrected right then on the air.

One appreciates their dilemma. The very medium of radio magnifies & intensifies political criticism. When such criticism reaches oral peoples orally, emotion & action are easily aroused, no matter how remote, or imperfectly understood, the issues.

Democracy takes many forms. But Western democracy is deeply rooted in literacy & not easily transposed into other media.

IDEAS LOOSE IN THE LAND

American slaves accepted Christian mythology as literally true, in part because it was printed in a book. Coming to them with all the freshness & immediacy any new medium always commands, the Bible enjoyed total acceptance.

Many New Guineans accept every radio program verbatim, no matter how mysterious, irrelevant, or conflicting. This is especially true of radio propaganda. Called by Americans "psychological broadcasts," some political programs are more psycho than logical—designed to reassure broadcasters, not convert listeners. Any political system that strives for rigid internal consistency runs the risk of madness; Voice of America & Peking Radio sometimes cross that threshold. Both broadcast in English—and in New Guinea, English is the prestige language. Radio lets villagers renew school-learned English. I observed young men in isolated villages listening intently to the wildest fantasies. When I talked to them about what they had just heard, or about things heard earlier, they offered literal interpretations, sometimes woven into the fabric of tribal beliefs, but more frequently unclassified.

Western listeners, long conditioned to hear radio as background sound, have little idea how extraordinary that same radio becomes when treated as foreground sound, that is, listened to intently & believed. As long as information is classified, it is controlled. But when it is unclassified, it is wild, unpredictable.

THEY RAVED, BUT THEY WERE NOT MAD

When radio hits oral, nonliterate peoples, it intensifies excitability. Villagers who once had no knowledge of what was happening in some distant capital, now receive that news daily in a form which makes it appear both urgent & relevant. But they cannot reply. Therefore they become at once more excited & more frustrated because nobody seems to be listening to them.

In 1969, the army was called out twice in one month, both times to deal with potential riots in communities where radio was part of daily life.

In Kieta, Bougainville, the immediate cause of unrest was the expropriation of land for a mining town. In Rabaul, New Britain, militant indigenes objected to expatriates serving in the legislature, though several had been democratically elected to do so. What followed was reported in detail by press & radio, including the international press. In fact, media coverage was so "hot," we refrained from filming either incident for fear the appearance of large cameras might increase the problem.

To government administrators, the response of the Kieta landowners was "unreasonable" & the position of the Rabaul militants was "irrational." If one accepted the complaints at face value, "unreasonable" & "irrational" were not unfair judgments. For the complaints, even if wholly true, didn't justify this sort of response. But this doesn't mean there weren't deeper causes.

Physicians speak of "referred pain," by which they mean pain felt as an area other than its source: e.g., a disorder of the kidney felt as pain in the arm.

I think the people of Kieta & Rabaul were making the only noises they knew to express the uncertainty inflicted on them by an alien culture & alien media. Since they had no anthropological vocabulary suitable to this misery, they used the vocabulary of the tribe & screamed nonsense about returning to tribal sovereignty because they recognized that their tribal life was doomed & with it all they treasured from the past.

WHY DIES HAS TO BE DULL

In broadcasting, the choice of motive is inescapable: power or profit. As Lyman Bryson notes, anyone who tries to escape this two-way choice by asking "Why shouldn't a mass medium be controlled by public interest?" is bound to say by whom the public interest is to be defined & this leaves him in the hands of government officials as before.

Profit can be concealed behind entertainment & power can be hidden behind dullness. Dullness is the ideal disguise. It makes power tolerable, even acceptable. This doctrine needs no enunciation or proclamation: it's an understood law of government operation.

Any government-owned medium becomes consciously an instrument of power. DIES is essentially a political instrument disguised as an educational & entertainment agency. But its power & dullness must coexist & compete with Australian Broadcasting Corporation, which aims toward pleasure. Competition between them blurs these differences (competition breeds similarity, not diversity) & each seeks to invade the domain of the other. But differences still exist. To appreciate these differences, one need only imagine the role DIES would play if it enjoyed a monopoly.

ABC is also a government agency, but an expatriate one, answering primarily to itself. Both by background & role,

ABC is far more professional & far more hospitable to talent than DIES. DIES's amateurism arises not from any limitations of staff, but as an inevitable condition of its role as a political instrument. In 1969, it regularly delayed broadcasting any criticism of government policy until the government had prepared a rebuttal—a rebuttal usually given more weight than the criticism.

The current two-agency system of broadcasting strikes me as ideal. I see no merit, least of all financial, in proposals to fuse these services. Nor do I see any merit in the current trend toward duplicating services, especially when the desirability of radically changing the acoustic environment of New Guinea seems unclear.

The problem: to maintain the existing agencies, furthering differences between them, while trying to prevent competition from making them alike.

Of course, these suggestions are made on the assumption & hope that political independence in Papua & New Guinea will not witness the abolition of ABC & DIES. If, however, the new political leaders use radio as a nationalized weapon to attack expatriates and as a political weapon to eliminate rivals, none of my suggestions are meaningful.

UNHOUSED

Paul Radin spoke of native autobiographies, but the term should be used with caution. Preliterate peoples don't write books or make films. We may train them to do so, but we must always ask: at this point, are they still members of their old culture or have they become, in this particular area at least, members of our culture?

I've recorded life histories extracted from informants. I've encouraged those who were literate to write their own. Since around 1960, I've put cameras in a variety of hands. The results generally tell more about the medium employed than about the cultural background of the author or cameraman.

In each case I had hoped the informant would present his own culture in a fresh way & perhaps even use the medium itself in a new way. I was wrong. What I saw was literacy & film. These media swallow culture. The old culture was there all right, but no more than residue at the bottom of a barrel. I think it requires enormous sophistication—media sophistication—before anyone can use print or film to preserve & present one's cultural heritage, even one's cultural present. The extraordinary sensitive autobiographies & films now coming out of Africa, come from men of the utmost media sophistication, men unhoused in any single culture or medium.

182

In New Guinea, we obtained about 70 films made by indigenes. Cameramen ranged in background from isolated Biami to Port Moresby students. Among isolated villagers, we ourselves became the subjects most frequently photographed, perhaps out of courtesy, more probably because we were the most visible objects in their environment. When we left cameras behind for them to use, they were generally ignored.

In Port Moresby, however, our cameras were in much demand. The subjects most favored were friends & cars. Cameramen might zoom & pan on scenery, but with friends & cars, they held the camera steady, preferably on a tripod: the cars they filmed were parked, the friends immobile. In other words, movie cameras were used like still cameras.

Four indigenes who worked with us (two in Port Moresby, one in the Sepik & one in the Highlands) became enthusiastic & competent filmmakers. They observed us closely, learned quickly & made films similar to the ones we were producing. None attempted to make the sort of dramatic films they saw in theaters, but I think if we had been shooting drama, they would have imitated this as well. In Angoram, we were asked to film dramatic skits staged by students & I noted that several skits might have been inspired by films.

I carefully screened films made by indigenous DIES cameramen. In only one did I see anything even remotely suggesting a nonWestern approach: a film on a *lakatoi*, a sailing ship, was exceptionally tactile, favoring close-ups of surfaces & bindings.

Western audiences delight in stories about natives who use modern media in curious ways, their errors being both humorous & profound, suddenly illuminating the very nature of the media themselves.

Even when these stories are true, I think their importance is exaggerated. Surely the significant point is that media permit little experimentation & only a person of enormous power & sophistication is capable of escaping their binding power. A very naive person may stumble across some interesting technique, though I think such stories are told more frequently than documented. The trend is otherwise.

New Guineans who may someday produce unique film statements, drawing upon their heritage & their contemporary lives, are almost certain to be men who were first dislodged from their native culture & then, by choice, returned to it, having acquired in the interval a knowledge of several media.

FEEDBACK

Our equipment suffered from humidity, forcing us to return every few months to Port Moresby where I had been appointed Research Professor, University of Papua & New Guinea.

The university is one of the finest I know. Competition for student admission is intense & opportunities for research & teaching attract superb faculty. The anthropology faculty is one of the best in the world. All its members engage in research & are much concerned with preparing students to assume leadership of their country.

This is also true of other faculties, for in New Guinea daily life is ethnographic. One political leader entitled his autobiography *Ten Thousand Years in a Life-Time*, a title applicable to the lives of many students. One instructor had a guesthouse for his students' parents. Using the students as interpreters, he recorded autobiographies of men born & raised in prehistory.

This was an ideal setting for dialogue, permitting me to discuss experiences & interpretations. Added to this, I was regularly interviewed over ABC radio. The resulting broadcasts were followed with interest throughout the Territory, so that almost everywhere we went, people discussed our work with us, often with keen insight & always with experience. I have never before enjoyed such feedback.

I didn't always experience this same feedback with government administrators, some of whom had never been out of Port Moresby. Those who had lived in villages—former missionaries, patrol officers, health officials—were often superbly observant, revealing great understanding of the very phenomena I sought to understand. But I found them reticent, either because they had ceased to find these phenomena remarkable, or because they sensed that their views would not be taken seriously. Certainly there was a widespread notion that observations & opinions in this field should come only from academically trained experts. No other voices were welcome.

In DIES, I met men who knew this land intimately & had observed, with wonder & insight, the effects of electronic media upon its people. Their views were nowhere taken seriously, not even by themselves. What was needed, I was constantly told, was someone like myself, with degrees, who knew how to conduct scientific research. DIES had several such studies on file, full of charts, statistics, jargon & incomprehensible descriptions of methodologies. I found them interesting only for what they revealed about the department. I was left with the impression that policy was an ephemeral thing, far removed from primary experience, made by men who combined strong, unexamined convictions with false notions about the nature of scientific inquiry.

The main effect of this insistence upon "scientific research" was to cut off intelligent feedback from the village level. It's ironic that this should have been done in the name of social science.

MISANTHROPOLOGY

Some years ago, Oliver LaFarge published a short story about an ethnologist who, as a young man, financed his studies among American Indians by collecting their treasures for museums. Over the years, his love of subject deepened to the point of identity, and toward the end of his life, he devoted much cunning to removing these pieces from museum storage & sending them back to their heirs. His actions came to light after his death when the Indian heirs again offered these pieces for sale.

The story is true. I knew him well. The dilemma he faced, anthropologists are only beginning to acknowledge. The truth is, though native informants may have liked anthropologists personally, they often distrusted their motives. Some suspected profits from books; others noted it was a paid job.

But what disturbed most was the feeling that when their dances & tales were filmed, taped & written down, they were stolen from them as surely as their lands & furs were taken away. When they saw their sacred treasures under glass, heard their songs on radio, watched their dances on TV, they not only objected to errors they spotted, they felt robbed. None of this had anything to do with them. They felt used. And they were.

The world's largest collection of primitive art was put

together by a man of great wealth & acquisitiveness who personally inked catalogue numbers on every specimen he bought, then stored these treasures in an inaccessible warehouse. The moment he catalogued a piece, it became his.

Anthropology, as an offspring of colonialism, reflects what Levi-Strauss calls "a state of affairs in which one part of mankind treats the other as object." The search for self-knowledge, which Montaigne linked to the annihilation of prejudice, has never been a dominant theme in 20th century anthropology. Not really. The trend has been toward the manipulation of peoples in the very course of studying them.

I don't refer to the close link between British anthropologists & the Colonial Office, or to American anthropologists working on CIA counterinsurgency projects. That was mere Winnie-the-Pooh.

I refer to the anthropologist's role as translator. Humane translation preserves & presents. Paul Radin insisted that the only acceptable ethnology was the life history, self-told by members of indigenous society. But those who undertook such efforts found themselves far removed from the mainstream of anthropology.

Even the concept of relativism has become, in the words of Stanley Diamond, "a perspective congenial in an imperial civilization convinced of its power. Every primitive or archaic culture is conceived as a human possibility that can be 'tasted'; it is, after all, harmless. We, at our leisure, convert the experience of other cultures into a kind of sport, just as Thorstein Veblen's modern hunter mimics, and trivializes, what was once a way of life. Relativism is the bad faith of the conqueror, who has become secure enough to travel anywhere."

Clothing themselves in liberal platitudes & employing what they called "scientific methodologies," anthropologists translated other cultures into unreadable jargon & statistics, almost none of it translatable back into life energy. They erased cultures with irrelevancy & dullness. A few ended up talking to each other in a language known only to themselves, about

189

subjects having no existence outside their closed circle. Little wonder informants felt shut out.

This was not true of a handful of reports published around the turn of the century. Publications of the Bureau of American Ethnology contained detailed, matter-of-fact, accurate descriptions of Zuni ceremonies, Hopi pottery designs, etc. These are used today as reference works by the Zuni & Hopi in their efforts to keep alive their heritage.

Almost nothing published in the last fifty years could serve that end. These later reports aren't repositories of knowledge; they're graves. No retrieval from them is possible.

Between 1946 & 1965, a typical research project began with a government grant & the assembly of an interdisciplinary team. Ideally, this included a psychologist, economist, etc., that is, representatives of categories meaningful to our culture, though alien to the culture studied. Generally no one was invited to participate who had shown prior interest in the subject, say someone who had learned the language of the subject group. The thought of including someone from the subject group itself never occurred.

If it was American Indians, reservations were taken as geographical locales, though for many Indians, social drinking-dancing clubs, which cut across Reservation lines & centered in cities, were primary. Time categories were based on government budgets, not indigenous calendars.

Every category came from the dominant culture. The indigenous culture wasn't preserved & presented: it was swallowed.

By the time administrators, missionaries, social workers & anthropologists got through with indigenous peoples, most were eager to forget their pasts. When "Dead Birds," a superb film on tribal warfare in New Guinea, was shown at the Administrative College, Boroko, one student angrily turned off the projector: "What right does anyone have to record what we choose to forget?" His statement was applauded.

The dilemma I faced in New Guinea was this: I had been asked to find more effective uses for electronic media, yet

190

I viewed these media with distrust. I had been employed by government administrators who, however well-intentioned, sought to use these media for human control. They viewed media as neutral tools & they viewed themselves as men who could be trusted to use them humanely. I saw the problem otherwise.

I think media are so powerful they swallow cultures. I think of them as invisible environments which surround & destroy old environments. Sensitivity to problems of culture conflict & conquest becomes meaningless here, for media play no favorites: they conquer *all* cultures. One may pretend that media preserve & present the old by recording it on film & tape, but that is mere distraction, a sleight-of-hand possible when people keep their eyes focused on content.

I felt like an environmentalist hired to discover more effective uses of DDT. There seemed no way to reach those who needed this information most. Even students at the University of Papua and New Guinea, though often sophisticated about the uses of media for political ends, still naively thought that when their images & words appeared within the media, this gave them public identity & power. They failed to grasp that this merely acknowledged their *existence* within these new environments; it is no way guaranteed them creative roles there. What was everywhere needed was the sort of media sophistication which comes only with detachment, dislocation, study. Such sophistication is not easily achieved.

I therefore decided that both the written report & film I produced would be addressed to no particular audience. Like the cry, "Fire!" I hoped they would receive the widest possible circulation & not just be heard by arsonists. This meant shunning "scholarly" publications, which have long since become a means of information control; it also meant avoiding conventional formats, another means of neutralizing information. Hence the format of this book.

Picture Credits

Frontispiece, Zuni katchina dolls: Edmund Carpenter. *Page 30*, Kuskomkwim Eskimo masks: Museum of the American Indian; The University Museum, Philadelphia, The Reis Family Collection. *Page 34*, New Britain, 1944, Marines jitterbugging: United Press International. *Page 46*, William Bligh: The New York Public Library; Charles Laughton as William Bligh: The Museum of Modern Art. *Page 49*, Lt. William Calley masks: Leonard Freed, Magnum. *Page 55*, audience viewing Rembrandt's "Aristotle Contemplating the Bust of Homer": Herbert Loebel. *Page 57*, Nigeria: Ken Heyman. *Page 87*, Chimbu, Highlands, New Guinea: Adelaide de Menil. *Page 122*, Congo figure: courtesy of The Brooklyn Museum, gift of A. and P. Peralta-Ramos. *Page 148*, Biami, Papua, New Guinea: Adelaide de Menil. *Page 163*, Earl Browder: United Press International; Senator Millard Tydings: United Press International; composite of Browder and Tydings: Enoch Pratt Library, Baltimore. *Page 166*, Chimbu, Highlands, New Guinea: Adelaide de Menil. *Page 183*, Telafomon, New Guinea: Adelaide de Menil.

DATE DUE

MAY 4 '82		
SEP 3 0 '86		
MAR 2 1 '89		
NOV		
APR 10		